# Truth-Based Learning

Also by Richard Stuby

*Declaration of the American Mind—America's True & Lasting Character*

# Truth-Based Learning

A Blueprint for
Personal Betterment & Human Flourishing

―――――

Richard Stuby

Copyright © 2024 Richard G. Stuby Jr.

Published in the United States by Jordan Ridge Press, an imprint of Jordan Ridge LLC, New Tripoli, PA.

Unless noted, all Scripture quotations taken from the (NASB®) New American Standard Bible®, Copyright © 1960, 1971, 1977, 1995, 2020 by The Lockman Foundation. Used by permission. All rights reserved. lockman.org

Truth-Based Learning™, Truth Practices Flow™, and the "head with divider" graphic are trademarks of Jordan Ridge LLC.

All rights reserved. No part of this book may be reproduced or transmitted in any form or by any means without written permission from the author.

ISBN 978-1-7347314-2-2

Library of Congress Control Number: 2024901691

Printed in the United States of America

For my children and posterity

# Contents

Note on Formatting ..................................................... i

Preface ................................................................ iii

Introduction ........................................................... 1

Goals of Learning ..................................................... 7

Setting the Stage for Truth ......................................... 11

Truth ................................................................. 21

Truth-Based Learning ................................................ 31

Operating Principles of Truth ....................................... 35

Natural Order Principles of Truth ................................... 49

Spiritual Order Principles of Truth ................................. 63

Truth-Based Learning Framework ...................................... 69

Truth Practices Flow ................................................ 73

Personal Betterment ................................................. 77

Human Flourishing ................................................... 109

The Source of Truth ................................................. 119

References .......................................................... 123

Biblical References ................................................. 129

Index ............................................................... 133

# Note on Formatting

Many terms in this book are used repeatedly in slightly different contexts. Formatting is used to help clarify word usage at any given time.

For example, "humility" is expressed in the following ways:

- As part of the Truth-Based Learning Framework diagram—*Humility*
- As an element of Truth-Based Learning—*humility*
- As a general principle, behavior, or practice—humility

Similarly, "truth," as the foundational concept of the book is expressed:

- As the overarching collection of all elements of truth—Truth
- As general usage of the concept of truth—truth

Concepts relating to Truth-Based Learning are capitalized when used as defined terms, such as Truth Behavior and Natural Order Principle, but may be used uncapitalized as general concepts.

In cases where the usage could apply to more than one meaning, the regular-text general usage is applied. Italics may also be used for definitions or emphasis.

Text in brackets [ ] may be added to quotations for clarity.

# Preface

I feel unworthy to define *Truth* and expound its principles and people's right behaviors in truth. I am a human with flaws, just like everyone else, and the topic regards the very foundations of human understanding. Yet, each human being that has ever lived, or ever will live, on this Earth must strive to learn and discern what is true and how to rightly apply truth, or resolve to live apart from Truth in ignorance. That being true, each of us now living is in a better position to reconcile with Truth than the great philosophers Aristotle, Marcus Aurelius, John Locke, Edmund Burke, and others, we having the advantage of their insights—and mistakes—and the intervening history against which to evaluate and discern truth, should we be wise enough to do so.

At the outset, my thought was that *Truth-Based Learning* would be a complete guide to learning, from philosophy of learning to curricula and support media. While these materials may flow from this effort in time, it seemed more prudent to not "bury the lede" of Truth-Based Learning in depths of pedagogy and productization, but rather to simply lay out the basics—*Truth-Based Learning* is a book of principles and behavioral practices that serve as guide rails for everyday living and personal betterment, in truth. If these take hold in someone's life, the goal is largely achieved. If they do not, added curricula or content would not really be of benefit.

As a result, the onus is on the reader to take direction from the structure of Truth-Based Learning and apply it to their own learning and to the education of others. This structure essentially enables a return to an earlier benchmark of learning when timeless truth was the guiding light. My hope is that people care enough to exercise Truth-Based Learning to maximize their personal potential and happiness and expand overall human flourishing for the benefit of others.

Richard Stuby

# Introduction

Truth-Based Learning is about enabling people to develop, endure, and thrive. This requires learning founded in truth—right learning—and continuous application of consistent principles and behaviors derived from Truth.

Truth is supreme. Without truth, there is no common basis for understanding among people. Without a common understanding, there can be no common learning. Without a common basis for learning, there can be no lasting community among people—it is impossible to accept existing knowledge without accepting it as being true. Without community, conflict is inevitable. Therefore, the basis of truth and the examination of truth are the most necessary premises of learning for the benefit of the individual and community.

Learning is individual assimilation, understanding, and application of knowledge. Education is the process by which learning is facilitated by someone other than the learner. All education is based in the doctrine of the educator. Unfortunately, educational doctrines may be strong or weak, just or unjust, true or false, in their position and purpose; and the lessons taught may be appropriate or inappropriate to the needs of a given student, and engaging or uninteresting in presentation to one or many students.

A right educational doctrine, one based in truth, will seek individual success and promote liberty while equipping the individual to benefit society. Misguided educational doctrine will limit individual liberty and success in the name of the "greater good" and mold the individual to serve the desires and dictates of societal authority. Unfortunately, individuals and families have ceded learning under right educational doctrine to institutional (public and private) education, which is continuously pressured to conform to popular culture and frustrated by myriad conflicting goals, most of which serve the objectives of societal authority and elitist planners but do little to serve the learner in achieving personal betterment. Additionally, institutional education is limited to doctrines promoting uniform learning across students and time. It evaluates student learning largely to demonstrate achievement of a minimal standard which provides little evidence of overall quality of education, and little affirmation of success to the high-achieving student. Given all of the variables, it seems unlikely that institutional education can produce a sound doctrine broadly favorable to everyone (or anyone).

Fallout from poor doctrine includes one-size-fits-all vocational education, targeting aptitude in the middle of the bell curve, intended to prepare students for mass employment for the benefit of societal and economic stability. This leaves the brightest and dullest learners to fend for themselves and leaves the middle echelon with a limited set of prescribed opportunities rather than supplying them with vocational options that support the pursuit of their talents and passions. Furthermore, learners at all levels are left without the skills necessary to develop knowledge, wisdom, and reasoning for individual betterment and inquiry into the structures of society and civilization that make human flourishing possible.

Institutional education has also usurped the mantle of parenting. Education is now deeply infused with "social" or "societal" goals that were once the sole province of parents. Many educational curricula now blend social-emotional learning theory (or the latest derivations and replacements) into all aspects of curricula, diminishing time on academic topics, focusing attention on the most disruptive students, and—under the guise of "socialization"—often promoting beliefs not held by parents, many not even held by society at large.

It becomes easy to understand why kids are bored with education in institutional classrooms. Essentially, they are being told that they must spend most of their youth being educated on subjects x, y, and z, then testing on them to demonstrate only minimal learning. All this so that they can join a "workforce" and slave away for the next 30 or 40 years at a job (more likely jobs), which they can only hope will meet their financial needs, and which they expect will not bring them happiness—and leaving them lacking the general learning needed to escape to better opportunity. The mantra of "Work hard and you can be whatever you want to be" just doesn't resonate and likely isn't true even if they believe it. The alternative to this "Suffer now so that you can suffer later" paradigm should be "Enjoy learning now so that you can enjoy life later" while at the same time being a valued and valuable part of society and human civilization.

Classical liberal education was the primary model of education that afforded this focus until being progressively abandoned over the past hundred-plus years. Journalist Toby Young defined it well,

> By a Classical Liberal Education we mean a rigorous and extensive knowledge-based education that draws its material and methods from the best and most important work in both the humanities and the sciences. The aim of such an education is not primarily to prepare pupils for a job or career. It is more to transform their minds so that they are able to make reasonable and informed judgments and engage fruitfully in conversation and debate—not just about contemporary issues,

but also about the universal questions that have been troubling mankind throughout history. (1)

Classical liberal education blends seamlessly with vocational education. There is no reason that someone who wants to make a living as a carpenter should be any less informed or wise than someone who wants to make a living as a rocket scientist. A wise carpenter can be a philosopher, a representative of the people, or a religious leader in addition to having their vocation.

Truth-Based Learning provides a pathway to this end, aligning with classical liberal education's goal of addressing universal questions. It is essentially a study on truth within the classical liberal sphere of learning, enabling right understanding of content within that sphere.

Learning, not education, is the goal of Truth-Based Learning. Education is *done to* a student; learning is *done by* the learner. A student may or may not be accepting of education, but a learner is, by definition, desirous of learning. Through learning, the learner can be discerning in what is valuable for all aspects of their education without needing jargon or expertise in the latest theories of education.

Truth-Based Learning enables parents of young learners to act more easily as the primary educators of their children or to become better advocates of their children's institutional education. It does not prescribe what facts or vocations to learn—those choices relate to individual interest and talent. Truth-Based Learning provides a blueprint for learning and a measuring stick for doctrines and curricula by which parents can act for their child's benefit and easily raise concerns with educators, administrators, school boards, and other parents.

Truth-Based Learning facilitates growth in the application of principles and practices leading to individual betterment and empowerment to seek one's full positive potential while providing guideposts and calling out pitfalls on paths one might take apart from truth. These same principles and practices are desirable for individuals, families, society, and civilization. This is because the principles that emanate from Truth are also the principles required for individuals and families to live in proximity to others—which is society—and are the principles required for civilization, which bolsters human flourishing. With human flourishing, individual opportunity grows and the virtuous circle repeats, civilization freeing and enabling more individual accomplishment which, in turn and in truth, advances civilization.

# Goals of Learning

Education cannot force learning, and while any number of people may be educated together, learning only occurs individually. Clearly, learning is important, and education is only important insofar as it successfully and rightly aids learning.

To rise to its level of importance, learning requires goals. Typical individual goals of learning include pursuing personal interests and making a wage to survive. Many governments and corporations view the end goal of learning to be socialization and a skilled workforce to fill jobs and grow the economy. However, parenting and economic stability are not the proper goals of learning. Rather, strong society and culture are the *result* of learning by which individuals live in liberty and respect the fundamental rights of others. Early American educational doctrine demonstrated this understanding under the premise that education is important to develop "wise and good" men and women (2), believing that wise and good citizens naturally serve society and thereby reinforce the stability of society. Roman emperor and Stoic philosopher Marcus Aurelius tacitly agreed with this premise of learning by noting the singular difference of a good man from other men:

> [T]he good man's only singularity lies in... his refusal to soil the divinity seated in his breast or perturb it with disorderly impressions, and his resolve to keep it in serenity and decorous obedience to God, admitting no disloyalty to truth in his speech or to justice in his actions. (3 p. 3.16)

It follows that there is a universal goal for learning that concentrates on individual needs and also incorporates societal needs. That goal is not learning *how to make a living*; it is, instead, learning *how to live* to best pursue and provide for one's own happiness. Addressed rightly, this universal goal of learning also means learning to live as the best person possible, with the broadest understanding and deepest wisdom possible. It entails developing personal meaning and purpose, gaining wisdom, developing character, living in liberty (avoiding tyranny, oppression, and slavery), and being enlightened to think and discern in order to maintain those qualities. It means to reach one's highest positive potential in life, not just to become a cog in a machine or a useless intellectual academic. As famous thinker Edmund Burke stated,

## Goals of Learning

> To study only for its own sake is a fruitless labour; to learn only to be learned is moving in a strange Circle. The End of learning is not knowledge but virtue; as the End of all speculation [contemplation] should be practice of one sort or another... Knowledge is the Culture [cultivation] of the mind; and he who rested there, would be just as wise as he who should plough his field without any intention of sowing or reaping. (4)

Through individual improvement, the condition of society is also improved, and through common understanding and (tacit) agreement or acknowledgment of certain principles of life, this benefit extends to broader civilization. Chief among those principles in common understanding is truth because untruth cannot lead to one's highest potential. Untruth breeds more untruth and, in the end, the house of cards of untruth becomes so tall and shaky that it falls with the addition of the smallest untruth. But in Truth, the house is laid on a firm foundation, and added levels tie into previous ones, making the structure able to withstand onslaught.

So, there is a need as part of human development to layer individual learning onto collected bodies of knowledge and wisdom from which others may learn. These bodies of knowledge and wisdom reduce the need for each generation to learn through rediscovery, allowing people to leverage the existing base to move forward with new learning. This creates a virtuous circle whereby personal betterment breeds collective improvement that increases the opportunity for greater and broader individual happiness.

American President Calvin Coolidge expressed this reality of truth being connected to learning with a civilization's body of knowledge, saying,

> We are to continue the guarantee of progress in the future by continuing a knowledge of progress in the past. We are to proclaim our allegiance to those ideals which have made the predominant civilization on earth. We believe that thought is the master of things. We realize that the only road to freedom lies through a knowledge of the truth. (5)

In the same address on education, Coolidge profoundly stated the relationship between human flourishing and learning,

> There has never been a great people who did not possess great learning. (5)

Ultimately, the goal of learning is living well in liberty according to one's desires and capabilities, striving for personal betterment, respecting the rights of others to do the same, and building relationships, resulting in a flourishing human civilization.

# Setting the Stage for Truth

Humanity is organized in societies—simple associations of mutual support for survival—and societies comprise civilizations, each with existing bodies of knowledge and diverse understanding of natural and spiritual things. Truth, more or less, intermingles these constructs within societies and civilizations, and they cannot continue long without it. Yet, humanity can only advance from its current state, whether the current state of humanity is standing in truth or not. Therefore, the question required to evaluate the condition of human organization is whether or not the understanding and application of truth within society and civilization is expanding or contracting.

## Civilization

Civilization is an advanced state of human development and collaboration beyond that of society. Without civilization, most of the goals of learning become moot, drowned in the ever-present challenge to survive and evade servitude. Without civilization, there is little chance for individual thriving and no chance for human flourishing.

Criteria signifying the existence of civilization include creation of wealth, division of labor, knowledge of science and engineering, development of cities, rise of social classes, political organization, robust literature and art, and foreign trade. These criteria demonstrate an expansion of human collaboration and societal development that permits human achievement to exceed subsistence or servitude. However, these are not criteria for generating civilization. Rather, they are some of the signs of *established* civilization.

Establishment of civilization requires consistent application of principles that define and protect the boundaries that sustain civilization and expand human opportunity. Civilization comes from societies minimally defined by a set of rules (law and culture) joining in unity of higher values—truth—for universal benefit.

Free Western Civilization best represents optimum civilization based in Truth. Western Civilization is the civilization born from Judeo-Christian principles, sustained in wisdom-minded Greek thought and democratic ideals, tempered under Roman law, and established in Roman peace (*Pax Romana*). Through the Renaissance and societal Enlightenment of Truth,

Western Civilization progressed from rule by kings to representative republican government by *The People*, culminating in the highest degree of individual liberty and human flourishing in history. Other societies claiming civilization have remained authoritarian or totalitarian, which has limited people's ability to know, understand, and exercise truth, thereby limiting achievement and limiting human flourishing—authoritarian or totalitarian "civilization" is only a shadow of free civilization, regardless of claims of being Utopia.

## Utopia

Sir Thomas More's 1516 book, *Utopia* (6), satirically describes the ultimate civilization. "Utopia" translates from Greek as "not a place." Yet, even within the satire, it depicts only a shadow of actual civilization because More's Utopia is authoritarian. In Utopia, there is no true liberty, arguably no love, and wisdom is misguided to an end of being for appearances to the outside world while complicit insiders are "happy" in continual fear of misstep, and the non-compliant become slaves for the "collective good."

## Natural and Spiritual Orders of Existence

There is a natural order and a spiritual order to human existence. The preamble of the United States' Declaration of Independence expresses this understanding as being foundational in American culture, using the labels *Laws of Nature* and *Laws of Nature's God*.

> When in the Course of human events, it becomes necessary for one people to dissolve the political bands which have connected them with another, and to assume among the powers of the earth, the separate and equal station to which **the Laws of Nature and of Nature's God** entitle them, a decent respect to the opinions of mankind requires that they should declare the causes which impel them to the separation. (7) (emphasis added)

This writing is derived from the Natural Law philosophy captained by John Locke, but the general concept applies to the understanding that people operate under a set of beliefs associated with the natural world around them and a set of spiritual or metaphysical beliefs beyond the physical realm. These metaphysical beliefs interact with, but do not necessarily align with the natural (for example, belief in life after death or belief in a conscience), but in aggregate, they form a complete system of human engagement with the world. Marcus Aurelius fundamentally agreed when he wrote,

> [K]eep your principles constantly in readiness for the understanding of things both human and divine; never in the most trivial action forgetting how intimately the two are related. For nothing human can be done aright without reference to the divine, and conversely. (3 p. 3.13)

These concepts of a natural order and a spiritual order in human existence are governed by principles that derive from Truth.

Natural order principles comprise reflexive or instinctive behaviors (as in rational *common sense*, not irrational animal instinct), which are required for people to live in proximity with one another. That is, natural order principles and behaviors enable society. A good example of a natural order principle is found in the biblical story of Cain's murder of his brother, Abel—the first murder in human history.

> [A]nd it happened that when they were in the field Cain rose up against his brother Abel and killed him. Then the LORD said to Cain, "Where is Abel your brother?" And he said, "I do not know. Am I my brother's keeper?" Then He said, "What have you done? The voice of your brother's blood is crying out to Me from the ground. Now you are cursed from the ground, which has opened its mouth to receive your brother's blood from your hand. When you cultivate the ground, it will

> no longer yield its strength to you; you will be a wanderer and a drifter on the earth." Cain said to the LORD, "My punishment is too great to endure! Behold, You have driven me this day from the face of the ground; and I will be hidden from Your face, and **I will be a wanderer and a drifter on the earth, and whoever finds me will kill me**." (Genesis 4:8-14) (emphasis added)

In his confrontation with God, Cain instinctively knows that murder is wrong and that the natural response to murder will be that others will seek to kill him, both to punish his transgression and for their own continuing safety. There is a natural order Justice that makes it readily understood that a murderer does not belong in society.

Spiritual order principles and behaviors are those that are beyond the natural. They are metaphysical, inspired by the Laws of Nature's God, acknowledging a "Power greater than ourselves" (as required in the Twelve Steps recovery process of Alcoholics Anonymous (8)). These spiritual beliefs may or may not be associated with formal religion, although the beliefs which have most significantly influenced the history of civilization have been. At its lowest limit, the spiritual order comprises the human capacity for self-awareness and self-reflection not present in any other creature.

The spiritual order of human existence is required for civilization. Where the natural order drives the basic structure to sustain society, the principles and practices of the spiritual order promote good individual character, which expands positive human interaction and relationships. These, being based in truth, permit sustainable and flourishing civilization. The Bible expresses this ancient understanding, highlighting that conscientious good behavior supersedes rote legal compliance:

> For when Gentiles [non-Jews] who do not have the Law [e.g. the Ten Commandments (Exodus 20:3-17)] instinctively perform the requirements of the Law, these, though not having the Law, are a law to themselves, in that they show the work of the Law written in their hearts, their conscience testifying and their thoughts alternately accusing or else defending them. (Romans 2:14-15)

## Body of Knowledge

Civilization provides people with a collected body of knowledge (*corpus scientiae*) to aid in learning. The body of knowledge leverages any manner of technology available from oral tradition to books in libraries to distributed resources accessible via the Internet. The quality of the civilization—the extent to which truth is valued—determines how well the body of knowledge is vetted for veracity. Not that it has been "fact-checked" by some anointed authority, or that it is sound based only in consensus—the "wisdom of crowds" (*argumentum ad populum* fallacy (9))—but that it has stood the test of time for reliability and conformity to truth. While the common sense of a sound *corpus scientiae* may seem to be the "wisdom of the crowd" assenting to its viability, it is, rather, the other way around—the crowd has assented to the body of knowledge because it is true and wise to do so.

The *corpus scientiae* advances the human condition by permitting society to build on past learnings, enabling growth in knowledge over generations, and obviating the need for each generation to relearn and reaffirm by experimentation. Without this history of knowledge, there would be no room for the development of civilization. In turn, individual learning that adds to the body of knowledge implicitly benefits society—"A rising tide lifts all boats." Better civilization then makes the body of knowledge more complete and more accessible, which in turn enables even better civilization. Individual learning and growing civilization are mutually supporting and sustaining. Conversely, ignorance breeds ignorance (as exemplified in the Dunning-Kruger effect), and a society not standing in truth corrupts the body of knowledge, diminishes the human condition, and requires civilization to be rebuilt from rehashed reason and experimentation, or dooms it if there is no change in respect of truth.

## Body of Wisdom

Beyond the scope of the body of knowledge is the body of wisdom (*corpus sapiens*), which directs the right application of the body of knowledge, lest it be easily corrupted, or its knowledge used out of context or for illicit, nefarious, or foolish purposes. This collection of persistent wisdom enables humanity to grasp the successes of past generations in knowing truth and provides added certainty that the facts of truth are used in proper context.

No one can know all subjects in the body of knowledge or comprehend all wisdom. Civilization trusts in the knowledge and wisdom of others who have come before to keep it in truth, the foundation of that trust being in the continuing existence of civilization itself. Without first examining the foundational contents of civilization's *corpus scientiae* and *corpus sapiens,* it is foolish to ask, "What is truth?" New generations can, and should, study that question in due course, but there exist tested answers for immediate application to living and continued learning. C.S. Lewis summarized the concept, stating,

> An open mind, in questions that are not ultimate, is useful. But an open mind about the ultimate foundations [of truth] is idiocy… Nor must we postpone obedience to a precept until its credentials have been examined. (10 pp. 48, 49)

## Common Sense

*Common sense* is the instinctive or conscience-based understanding of basic truths that have been tested through time, like "water will wet" and "fire will burn" (11). It is, as derived by C.S. Lewis,

> [T]hings so obviously reasonable that they neither demand nor admit proof. (10 p. 40)

Common sense is "common" in being fundamental and foundational, not because of universal acceptance. Popular culture plays a significant role in the acceptance and understanding of common sense at any given time in a society.

Usage of the term *common sense* is often abused by labeling a position in an argument as being common sense to escape the need to actually defend the argument, or in an effort to gain endorsement from uncritical onlookers who are unwilling to seek the truth of the matter. Just because someone describes their point as being common sense does not make it common sense, and just because the majority believes something is true does not necessarily make it so.

# Truth

Truth is the way things are—the preternatural, eternal, and enduring foundation of all things.

According to the philosopher Aristotle,

> [T]he principles of eternal things should be *always* most true; for they are not *sometimes* true, nor is any thing the cause of being to them, *but they are the causes of being to other things*, And hence, such as is the being of every thing, such also is its truth. (12)

Truth is supreme, above all other principles, and unchangeable. If truth were changeable with respect to being, truth would also be changeable with respect to truth (itself) and, therefore, could not be truth. Aristotle confirms this understanding by stating that "principles of eternal things should be always most true." If then, there are eternal principles that are "most true," those principles must be the principles by which to live.

Aristotle defined truth this way:

> For to say that being is not, or that that which is not is, is false; but to affirm that being is, and that non-being is not, is true. (13)

Aristotle understood that the opposite of truth is untruth, or falsehood. Therefore, if, as Aristotle also recognized, truth is the foundation for eternal principles, then falsehood corrupts eternal principles—falsehood is wicked; truth is righteous and good. Truth and falsehood are incompatible. One not accepting truth is denying or defying it. This insight is confirmed in biblical principles: "The tree is known by its fruit, good or bad, but not both." (Matthew 12:33). "A kingdom divided against itself cannot stand." (Matthew 12:25). "The one not living in truth is living against the truth" (Matthew 12:30).

Frederick Douglass, the escaped slave turned self-educated philosopher and advocate for liberty and equality, spoke of truth and untruth (the latter of which he labeled *error*) during the American Civil War:

> Indeed, I ought to state, that what must be obvious to all, that, properly speaking, there is no such thing as new truth; for truth, like the God whose attribute it is, is eternal. In this sense, there is, indeed, nothing new under the sun. Error may be properly designated as *old* or *new*, since it is but a misconception; or an incorrect view of the truth. Misapprehensions of what truth is have their beginning and their

endings. They pass away as the race move onward. But truth is 'from everlasting to everlasting,' and can never pass away. (14)

In this light, truth may also be understood by examples of what it is not. Truth is not democratic. Truth is not determined by consensus. There is no separate "my truth" and "your truth." The intensity of one's beliefs does not make them true. There may be different beliefs as to what is truth, but the truth is not moved by beliefs. Truth is not changed by culture, even if culture changes the popularity of truth. Truth affords no prerogative; it applies universally to all. Truth is not created by mankind; it exists—it is an "eternal thing," as expressed by Aristotle.

---

### Aristotle

Aristotle was a Greek philosopher living from 384 to 322 BC. Universally viewed as one of the greatest philosophers of all time, Aristotle is placed in the company of Plato, at whose academy he studied, and Socrates, who taught Plato.

---

## Importance of Truth

Truth is eternal and good. Truth is the foundation of the principles by which to live. Therefore, the principles by which to live always align with goodness. This is the importance of Truth—it enables individual human enlightenment and the ability to live well. However, humans are social creatures, and Truth recognizes the social need of humanity and requires interdependence between individuals for them to thrive. Therefore, individual enlightenment in a vacuum is of little value, and the importance of truth extends beyond the individual to the benefit of society and civilization—without truth, there is no common basis for understanding and community among people. Civilization, in turn, is important because, operating in truth, it nurtures human flourishing by providing a stable foundation for individuals living from one day to another—in the family, with friends, and in society under law and culture.

## Discovery of Truth

Truth may be found in the everyday world, discovered through experience, reason, and intuition. Time moves forward. Life has value. Water is wet and fire will burn. To say of these that they are not, is false. To say of these that they are, is true.

Truth becomes evident when pursued diligently. Yet, truth exists whether it is known or not, just like scientific facts exist before they are discovered. And truth overarches the capacity of science as implied in the United States' Declaration of Independence:

> We hold these **truths to be self-evident**, that all men are created equal… (7) (emphasis added)

It is unnecessary to scientifically test the equality of mankind (if it could even be tested and determined to be scientific law), but the common sense of nature testifies to it, and intuition accepts it as truth.

The basic relationships required for community and society rely on a common basis for understanding under Truth. Therefore, there must be a foundation of unchanging, agreed (at least assented) truth for a society or civilization to be sustainable. Within civilization, most truth is learned from the collected body of truth that undergirds that civilization, having been cataloged through the trials and errors of societies over time. This timeless truth is akin to a statement of faith. It is apprehension and acceptance of tested and enduring knowledge and wisdom, even though they may be unprovable. As discerned by C.S. Lewis, "If nothing is self-evident, nothing can be proved." (10 p. 40) Thus, the truth of a free civilization is longstanding and robust, and rapid or wholesale departure from accepted truth is foolishness, leading to the downfall of civilization and to individual suffering.

The value of truth must be recognized before expending the effort to pursue truth. This reality may seem a bit of a paradox, but the same basic requirement is needed before pursuing anything—no one digs for gold without first valuing it. However small or fleeting the event, everyone experiences truth, and falsehood, and (almost) everyone recognizes the benefit of truth over falsehood. Once recognized, some will pursue truth to their betterment while others will live apart in unspoken acknowledgement of it, to their detriment.

> ## Science
>
> Science is the study of the detectable world, expanding knowledge through the use of the scientific method. The scientific method is the process by which observable world (natural order) questions are tested and best understood. Science is not truth, although it often helps to uncover truth. The scientific method can be improperly implemented, misused, or self-fulfilled, thereby corrupting scientific knowledge. Therefore, good science requires discernment through philosophy, reason, and logic to properly serve Truth. There is no proven science—the closest thing to proof in science is a *scientific law*, and many theories deemed to be scientific law are shown to be false or incomplete under extended scientific scrutiny.

## Defense of Truth

Because falsehood exists in opposition to truth, and truth is needed for a thriving human condition, there is a need to defend truth from falsehood. Truth is always under attack from forces seeking to benefit from ignorance, anarchy, and authoritarianism. Truth is usually assaulted surreptitiously by infecting culture or law, inducing a person or a society to trip and stumble into falsehood, rather than making an open assault on truth. However, when the defense of truth wanes as the influence of falsehood in culture and law mounts, attacks on truth become open and bold. In such times, the wicked become so bold as to call truth untruth and untruth truth.

In open untruth, love may be misappropriated, calling brutality romance, and calling romance unconditional love. Personal preference may be labeled wisdom, making wickedness honorable and calling foolishness discernment. Gratitude and virtue may become tools of vanity, twisting caring behaviors into causes for pride and demands for respect. Duty may become a curse, and licentiousness labeled liberty. Vengeance may become justice, and mercy only a call for a bribe. The worst behaviors of mankind may become known as goodness and excellence—because untruth holds no bounds. Humankind needs to protect truth from being overwhelmed by falsehood by exposing untruth and behaving in truth to avoid detriment of individual enlightenment and to halt dilapidation of society and civilization.

## Summary – Core Principles of Truth

Truth is the supreme principle directing "the principles of eternal things (12)," which are righteous. Without truth, all other principles are merely flawed preferences ("error," as Frederick Douglass called it). Truth is discoverable through experience, reason, and intuition, leading to wisdom and opportunity and to the enablement of society and civilization through enlightened human relationships. However, falsehood exists in opposition to truth, and there are some who choose the foolishness, ignorance, and wickedness of untruth over the enlightenment and opportunity of truth. Therefore, to best aid living in truth and avoid the deception and misery of falsehood, one must continually and openly seek and learn truth. This learning may be accomplished through practice of the principles of eternal things that are directly achievable in everyday life.

## Falsehood

The main manifestations of falsehood are foolishness, ignorance, and wickedness. Foolishness—intrinsically the opposite of wisdom—is acting apart from the right application of truth. Unintentional foolishness is ignorance. Ignorance is consumed with itself and cannot, or will not, seek the truth. Like a blind squirrel, ignorance may occasionally find an "acorn" of truth, but it thrives on meeting its own desires and will sacrifice truth at any turn. Proverbs of the Bible says, "A fool does not delight in understanding, but in revealing his own mind" (18:2) and "He who trusts in his own heart is a fool" (28:26) and "The wise will inherit honor, but fools increase dishonor" (3:35). Following this pattern, ignorance breeds ignorance, which leads to willful ignorance and wickedness. Wickedness hides the truth, leverages falsehood, and attempts to pervert or disparage truth for its own purposes. No individual can thrive in ignorance, and no society or civilization can stand long in wickedness.

## Facts vs. Truth

Facts—proven knowledge, insofar as something is provable—are not the same as truth. Facts and science do not make truth; they only provide a means to uncover truth. Facts can be used in disinformation, but truth exposes disinformation.

However, fact and truth are often equated in everyday language. The assertion that diamond is a form of carbon can be shown via the scientific method to be *fact* for an individual diamond. That every diamond that has ever been evaluated has shown to be carbon constitutes a scientific law. If every diamond across time could be evaluated and shown to be carbon, then the assertion would also be a discrete factual element of Truth. We assume (discern) this would be the case and accept as truth the statement (believe it) that diamond is a form of carbon. Such wisdom makes everyday life tenable, enabling human flourishing rather than causing societal paralysis by requiring every fact to be continually reestablished in truth. That noted, as with common sense, the presumption of facts can lead to the abuse of truth. Even if knowable, the totality of discrete facts would still not comprise the totality of Truth because much of truth is spiritual or beyond current understanding, untestable by the scientific method.

# Truth-Based Learning

Truth-Based Learning supports the goals of learning by pursuing truth and its foundations for self, society, and civilization, then deriving principles, purposes, and practices by which one can learn, grow, and live in truth. It also reduces the need for the social indoctrination and remedial emotional development prevalent in so much of today's institutional education.

Truth-Based Learning extends (or restores) these desired outcomes of learning by focusing on Truth and its subordinate principles and behaviors to provide the foundation by which one may more easily and rightly learn. For this, Truth-Based Learning provides a framework of principles and practices, leaning heavily on truth tested in the foundation of Western Civilization, understood through culture, religion, and government, because no other civilization has so vastly enabled freedom, encouraged personal betterment, and supported individual prosperity while simultaneously broadening human flourishing.

Truth-Based Learning is for everyone, regardless of career interest or talent. Its principles and practices are equally accessible and attainable for everyone. However, assent to the supremacy of truth and understanding of the tools that civilization provides to engage the future are necessary to make use of Truth-Based Learning.

It is challenging for people to determine what is and what is not truth in every instance and issue in life. Fortunately, Truth has subordinate principles which break Truth down to manageable principles for living. Referring to the High-Level Structure of the Truth-Based Learning Framework (page 34), just below the foundation of *Truth* are the *Operating Principles of Truth*. The operating principles are the major modes by which truth functions in a real and tangible way. They are also principles by which the truthfulness of a situation can be assessed.

With the *Operating Principles of Truth* in place, the next level of Truth Principles may be positioned to their left and right in the diagram. The *Natural Order Principles of Truth* and the *Spiritual Order Principles of Truth* are relational principles feeding from, and governed by, the operating principles. These principles leverage the concepts of natural and spiritual orders of existence and highlight, respectively, the principles required to live in society and those required for civilization and human flourishing. They provide the granularity of truth needed to address learning and life situations with specific actions and behaviors. Flowing from the *Natural Order Principles of Truth* and *Spiritual Order Principles of Truth* are the *Truth Behaviors*.

Subsequent chapters will address in detail the Operating Principles of Truth, the Natural Order and Spiritual Order Principles of Truth, and the Truth Behaviors leading to a complete detailed framework for Truth-Based Learning. Ultimately, the Truth Behaviors of the framework will become learning practices—Truth Practices—grouped by purpose to enhance their applicability to common circumstances and enabling the alignment of everyday life with the principles of Truth. In short, the Truth Practices lead to the end game of Truth-Based Learning—personal betterment and loving human relationships.

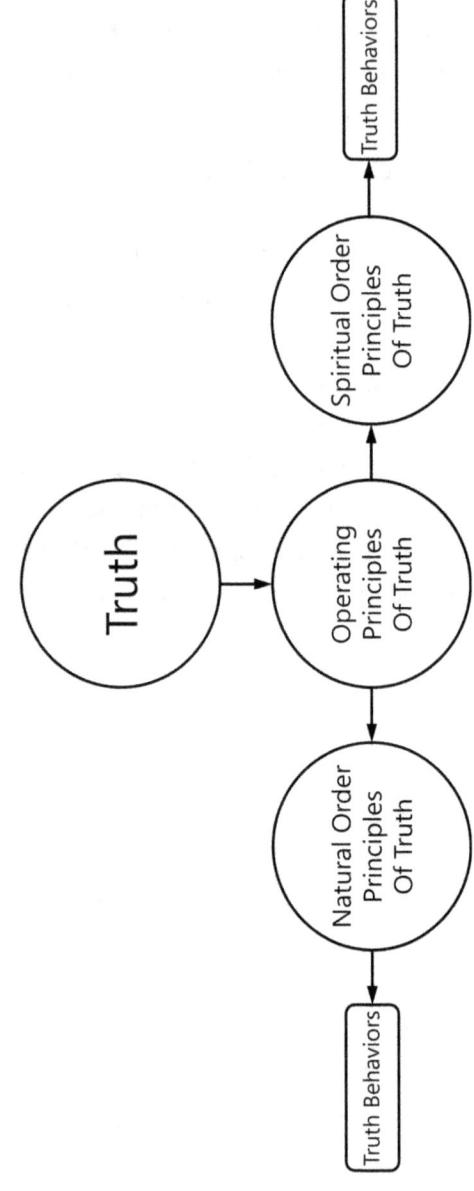

# Operating Principles of Truth

Because truth is good, the subordinate principles of Truth—*love* and *wisdom*—are also good. If the truth one believes does not develop and sustain love and wisdom, and uphold the principles that derive from them, then that "truth" is not *the Truth* and must be discarded for right principles and behaviors that align with truth. *Love* and *wisdom* are the operating principles by which truth may be translated into action and further refined into learning for individual betterment and human flourishing.

## Love

Love is the proper foundation of all human relationships. Love inspires gratitude and duty, and underpins virtue and mercy, all of which attend to the goodness of truth.

The English language is very simplistic when it comes to the word *love*. I *love* my wife. I *love* my mother. I *love* my friends. I *love* my dog. I *love* my pickup truck. And I *love* myself. These simple sentences are the same except for the object of my love, and they all convey a different level of relationship, expressed as love, with those objects. I love my wife—with her I have an intimate bond, special respect, and friendship, and I am willing to sacrifice my life for her. I love my mother—I respect and love her as my parent and have gratitude for all she has done for me. We share friendship, and my willingness to sacrifice for her has grown as I have aged. I love my friends—with them I have a bond of friendship. I am willing to sacrifice for them but more hesitantly than for my family members. I love my dog—I reciprocate the loyalty that he gives to me, and I care about his happiness and well-being. I love my pickup truck—I enjoy how it looks and rides and the utility that I gain from having it. I love myself—I take care of myself, and I am happy with most of my thoughts and actions, and I strive to improve the ones I don't like. Although all these relationships and affections are generally good, and despite calling all these sentiments *love*, they are not all the same.

Love is not one emotion. In fact, the highest forms of love are not emotions at all but willful actions. The Greek language is much more expressive about *love* than English and provides a means to understand these distinctions by categorizing *love* in five forms: *agape*, *philia*, *eros*, *storge,* and *philautia*. *Agape* and *philia* are spiritual types of love. *Eros* and *storge* are physical, or emotional, types of love. *Philautia* is a cultural type of love.

## *Agape*

*Agape* is sacrificial love, the highest form of love. *Agape* is learned, reasoned, or inspired. Its selfless nature implies that it must be personally chosen, denying oneself in favor of another. As much as someone loves a pet or a pickup truck, that sentiment is not *agape*. *Agape* is willful human love, one person to another, giving in abundance and considering the other person as better than oneself, which requires spiritual introspection. The Bible, in the words of Jesus and the apostle Paul, denotes *agape* as the highest form of love by describing it in action and affirming its relationship with truth and opposition to wickedness (each use of *love* in the quotations is *agape* in the original Greek):

> "Greater love has no one than this, that a person will lay down his life for his friends." (John 15:13)

> Love is patient, love is kind, it is not jealous; love does not brag, it is not arrogant. It does not act disgracefully, it does not seek its own benefit; it is not provoked, does not keep an account of a wrong suffered, it does not rejoice in unrighteousness, **but rejoices with the truth**; it keeps every confidence, it believes all things, hopes all things, endures

all things. (1 Corinthians 13:4-7) (emphasis added)

## *Philia*

*Philia* is brotherly love. *Philia* is learned or reasoned love toward family, friends, and even strangers—the kind of love that leads one to care for an injured stranger or help someone change a flat tire without obligation or desiring anything in return. *Philia* is spiritual love, characterized by less devotion than *agape* but, like *agape*, requiring a choice and cultivation to develop the principle into action.

Marcus Aurelius observed this concept, stating,

> In accordance with Nature's law of brotherhood I am to deal amiably and fairly with [others]. (3 p. 3.11)

## *Eros*

*Eros* is emotional love—the physical attraction for, and desire to be with, another person. *Eros* is not achieved through intimate contact—sexual intercourse is not love. Rather, intimate contact results from *eros*. *Eros* is romantic love which rightly should be grounded in spiritual love, becoming an extension of *philia* and *agape*. Without a bond to selfless love, *eros* becomes not love but infatuation or lust, seeking only self-satisfaction.

## *Storge*

*Storge* is instinctive or natural affection having the appearance of higher love. *Storge* may be considered the animal version of *philia* without the reasoned choice that is part of *philia*. A mother hen caring for her chicks demonstrates *storge*. A zebra facing a lion to save its colt shows *storge*. This innate affection is also present between humans, parent and child, and sibling to sibling, especially when young, as well as being present in dutiful devotion or caring for others.

## *Philautia*

*Philautia* is self-love, and there is much room to consider that it is not love at all because *philautia* can just as easily be viewed as vanity, which is a vice and a character flaw. Aristotle is often poorly translated and quoted out of context as a means to suggest that self-love comes before and above love of others. The popular statement, "All friendly feelings for others are an extension of a man's feelings for himself" is better translated as,

> The feeling of friendship towards friends, and those which distinguish the different kinds of friendship, seem to be derived from the feelings of a man toward himself. (15)

This translation allows little room for the interpretation of placing self-love above love of others, instead discerning that the quality of relationships flows from the effort placed in developing them. This idea is further upheld by noting that Aristotle goes on to discuss that this derivation of feelings stems from a good man's desire for good and virtue in relationship.

The Bible shuns self-love, associating it with traits like covetousness and ingratitude, but elsewhere notes that no one ever hated his own body but rather nourishes and cherishes it. It also instructs one to "love your neighbor as yourself," implying that *philautia* should be good and caring like *agape*. Given this, and the right understanding of Aristotle that a person's self-love must be based in seeking to do good, there seems to be room for cultural acceptance of *philautia* as a type of love, with the strong caution and cultural backstop that it be kept in alignment with, and in subordination to, the other classifications of love.

Love is what binds humanity. All other relationship drivers eventually fail. This is why *love* is an Operating Principle of Truth. Without love, all human relationships are based merely in transactional value subject to constant mistrust and calculated behavior. Without love there can be no forbearance or forgiveness of another, and therefore, no lasting peace. *Philia* and *agape* are the human characteristics, developed by rational choice, which enable mankind to move beyond the Law of Nature, to live fruitful and meaningful lives, to create, to progress in knowledge and wisdom, and to have relationships with each other and with God.

Human love begins with *storge*, the instinctive affection of a child for its parent. Learning through natural example within relationships and via instruction on proper behavior toward others, *storge* progresses to *philia* and, in the best case, to *agape*. There is, however, no certainty in these lessons occurring or being learned, which is a reason why there are many broken people in the world. It also highlights why the nuclear family—a father, mother, and children—is so important to the development of the individual human condition in society and civilization. Families provide the best agency for demonstrating and growing love, perpetuating a virtuous circle of truth across generations. Love begets love. Love grows through interaction of parent to child, sibling to sibling, grandparent to child within a family. Learning how to love then moves to love for friends and neighbors and community, until love becomes the norm for civilized people, and the cycle is mutually reinforced from individual to community and back again. Truth is also reinforced as love becomes the desire of civilized people because love overcomes the offenses that obscure truth. So, truth empowers love, assures it, and reinforces the actions and principles flowing from it, and love for others leads people to seek the truth.

There is a saying that "It takes a village to raise a child." This is untrue. It takes love to raise a child, and a village is raised and sustained through loving families and neighbors. Raised without love, individuals are challenged to learn the lessons of *philia* and *agape*, and the community suffers for it in a vicious cycle of decline rather than a virtuous circle of flourishing.

## Wisdom

*Wisdom* often evokes thoughts of majestic orators spouting profound pronouncements with grand gestures. But wisdom is simply the right application of truth and knowledge. Therefore, wisdom is right understanding. Having wisdom, one is less likely to be fooled or misled and more likely to obtain security, prosperity, and happiness.

Too often in society, wisdom is supplanted by the whims of "influencers" and the agendas of "experts." Typically, "influencers" are celebrities whose only qualification to guide the masses is the ability to draw enough attention to themselves by any means—foolishness, sexuality, comedy, fame, or perversion—to sway people's emotions and beliefs to some "narrative" that suits the wants of those who compensate the influencer. "Experts" are those credentialed in some (often impractical or contrived) academic specialty, biased by foolish doctrines, and compromised by the desire to control others. "Experts" profess beliefs with religious conviction but do not question, or allow others to question, their learning. In so doing, "experts" become the tools of confidence schemers ("con men"), elitist manipulators, and power brokers, like *The Media,* who promote them as the sanctioned source of truth on whatever topic relates to their supposed expertise. In the end, without wisdom in truth, these "experts" are no more than publicly endorsed influencers peddling their wares for a payout, power, or fifteen minutes of fame.

There is no wisdom in seeking self-justification as an "influencer" or "expert," or to follow such people, because wisdom is always justified by its alignment with truth. It is better to be wise and aligned with truth than to be an unwise "influencer" or "expert" accepted in the moment, but eventually ignored or castigated when truth is revealed.

## *Discernment*

*Discernment* is an element of *wisdom*, providing the ability to separate truth from untruth—the "right" in "right application" of truth. It is the ability to identify falsehood and wickedness and to know goodness. Lack of discernment leads to deception. The natural order operator of discernment is reason, and the spiritual order operators are conscience, intuition, and inspiration.

Discernment requires one to set aside desires for self and others to perceive and acknowledge truth. Discernment then ensures that Truth Practices remain positive and good, protecting them from drifting into foolishness and wickedness. For example, by discerning that a "too good to be true" financial offer is a scam, one can decline it, avoid loss, and be content in knowing that no wonderful opportunity was missed.

Discernment benefits from practicing reasoning through critical thinking and in developing wisdom through Truth

Behaviors. However, discernment can be a challenging principle to command in practice because it is often not formulaic in practice—there is no formula for intuition—and is easily clouded by pride, lust, jealousy, selfishness, biases, and other foolish and wicked behaviors. One might be able to say, "I will practice gratitude today," with some expectation of success in demonstrating humility or compassion, but it is more challenging to say, "I will practice discernment today," being sure that truth will be rightly perceived.

## Reason

Contemporary understanding of reason leans toward specific uses of process, like the scientific method or a mathematical proof. These processes are a subset of the broad base of the philosophical reason advanced by Aristotle, Marcus Aurelius, and John Locke, but they are far from the fullness of reason.

Locke highlighted the importance of reason with the statement,

> Reason, which God hath given to be the Rule betwixt Man and Man. (16)

By "rule," Locke invokes the Laws of Nature and Nature's God, rationale that is searchable and knowable so that by using reason an outcome under Truth may be discerned.

In a similar vein, Marcus Aurelius wrote,

> Reason, and the act of reasoning, are self-sufficient faculties, both inherently and in the method of their operation. (3 p. 5.14)

Reason is intended to be a path to wisdom for application of truth in human relationships in order to avoid dealing in foolishness, ignorance, and wickedness.

## Media and Influencer Narratives

*The Media* is the Internet-age term for the storytellers and commentators that have supplanted journalism and commercial network news as the broadly accepted source of current events, culture, and information. The change in label arose as journalism moved from presenting largely unbiased information to presenting *narratives*—stories that align with a goal irrespective of alignment with truth—as unbiased fact. Gone are most independent, truth-seeking, and unbiased information sources. Therefore, media content should always be scrutinized for "priming," which is the twenty-first century method of disseminating propaganda.

## Critical Thinking

*Critical thinking* is a popular term for problem solving. It has origins more than a hundred years old with the goal of developing a scientific attitude in education (17). However, because its theory is based in attitude of mind, and not process, its definition, applicability, and value vary by proponent and practitioner. At the core of the beneficial behaviors of critical thinking are inquisitiveness, thoroughness, and open-mindedness in evaluating available information to solve a problem or achieve a goal (the creativity and freedom of liberty aids critical thinking). Unfortunately, formal critical thinking proponents generally encourage the "thinker" to lean heavily on subjective personal beliefs in the practice, often leading to an incorrect or suboptimal solution bounded by their existing knowledge and wisdom. Despite the reticence of educational philosophers to assign a process to critical thinking, and apart from flaws in academic theory, practical *critical thinking* should be considered a blanket term for using logic, reasoning, inference, deduction, scientific method, mathematical proof, iteration, etc., as well as truth, wisdom, and discernment for developing the correct, or best, conclusion to a problem or decision.

# Natural Order Principles of Truth

Natural order principles are reflexive and instinctive, providing the natural basis for people to live together in mutual benefit. The Natural Order Principles of Truth, operating through *love* and *wisdom*, are *duty* & *liberty*, *justice* & *mercy*, and *equality*.

## Duty & Liberty

*Duty* and *liberty* form an inseparable dyad under Truth, with *culture* at their intersection. Neither principle can rightly function without the other. Where duty overwhelms liberty, personality and creativity are challenged and human flourishing suffers for lack of individual expression, variety, and innovation. The result is a bland existence of conformity under duty. Where liberty overwhelms duty, licentiousness—lack of legal and moral restraint—reigns, and truth quickly yields to foolishness and wickedness. Culture is the bellwether of the balance between duty and liberty.

## Duty

Duty—that natural duty coming from Truth—is guided by *storge* love, instinctive and innate. Duty's key nature being that it—through the Truth Behavior, *dutifulness*—chooses to sacrifice elements of individual liberty for relationship with others, comprehensive of natural obligation to help and defend others, as a means to support everyone.

The other type of duty, cultural or civil duty, is not based in love and truth, but is coerced or indoctrinated by human authority to curtail individual liberty and exert control. For example, in World War II, Japanese soldiers were duty-bound to their emperor—he being deemed a god—to die fighting, even in futility, or to take their own lives rather than surrender and dishonor him.

The real distinction between true duty and cultural duty is the informed and free attitude of the doer. Right duty is driven by truth, with love. Any "duty" that is forced or requires neglect or diminution of truth is not right duty. Also, right duty should not be confused with loyalty. Loyalty is a behavior, not a principle, and, like cultural duty, may be wrongly practiced.

Military service provides examples of both types of duty. For one person, military service may be a matter of duty based in truth because it is voluntary, an act of sacrificial love for country and countrymen; yet for another person, military service may be a matter of civil duty, only undertaken because of cultural pressure or under force, such as by conscription.

> ## Loyalty
>
> Loyalty—personal faithfulness—is an honorable behavior when motivated by proper duty and gratitude. However, misguided loyalty can also be driven by fear, lust, or desire for power. In wickedness, loyalty can even lead one to murder. Therefore, the value of loyalty is best left for consideration in specific circumstances rather than framing it as a virtue and then exempting the many possibilities under which it can be construed as bad behavior.

## Liberty

The principle of *liberty* practiced in righteousness derives from *wisdom*. Liberty apart from duty and wisdom ends in licentiousness. So, while liberty in both righteousness and licentiousness entails self-expression and self-satisfaction, only liberty enjoyed in wisdom and checked by duty is right behavior backed by truth.

Liberty is more than just a tame version of licentiousness. Liberty provides respite from the demands of other principles of living, allowing people to exercise individuality and creativity. This promotes individual well-being and protects society from unmitigated "duty" that leads to subjugation. Liberty also catalyzes excellence, making pursuit of excellence enjoyable because it is freely chosen.

The self-centered nature of liberty also presents opportunity for self-reflection, encouraging recognition of the rights of others. The *Golden Rule* which states, "Treat people the same way you want them to treat you," is reflected in the exercise of liberty as "Leave me to do as I wish and I will leave you to do as you wish," to which duty adds, "and we will abstain from conflict and wickedness." However, untruth is not equal in value to truth. Therefore, the related maxim, "Live and let live" is only rational when based in truth, properly reading as, "Live in truth and let live in truth." Put another way, liberty recognizes everyone's rights—yours and others'—where rights are simply the categorization of behaviors that are supported in liberty by truth.

## Culture

Culture reflects the collective balance of liberty and duty in society, which defines the values of a society and reveals the vigor of a civilization. An expanding civilization exists in a culture of liberty and justice in truth, and a declining civilization attempts to persist in a culture of licentiousness, perverted justice, and wickedness.

In practice, at any given time, there tend to exist two versions of culture within society, the foundational culture and the popular culture (pop culture), jointly defining the *zeitgeist*. The foundational culture is like the water level in a lake on a clear day. It is flat and extends across the whole lake. Popular culture is like the waves on the lake driven by passing winds. The waves rock boats, erode shorelines and splash in all directions as the inlets, bays, and depths allow, until the weather passes. Like the varying effects of the waves, individual experiences in popular culture differ, and the foundational culture remains even when the effects of popular culture are significant. The foundational culture can only change through concerted effort—plugging the spring that feeds the lake or breaching the dam that establishes the water level.

Popular culture has a place in individual expression and collective exploration of truth, but the mistake regularly made in humanity's limited horizon of thought is believing that popular culture is the norm rather than a temporary aberration producing exploration and learning, but never lasting (or leading to calamity if it does). In this error, foolishness and falsehood may become viewed as "new" truth, damaging society and civilization until love, wisdom, and discernment return collective thoughts to truth.

> ### Benefits of Liberty
>
> Liberty activates special individual attributes—*personality* and *creativity*. Liberty is the predominant conduit for individual expression and individual impact on society and civilization. Personality is an input to liberty. One's personal characteristics—whether through nature or nurture—direct how one acts in liberty (including the degree to which duty is valued). One's personality in liberty, then, produces individual effects captured in aggregate as creativity—the "salt" that seasons one's actions beyond simple duty. Creativity is impossible where there is no liberty. A prisoner breaking rocks all day and chained in a cell all night has no ability for creativity (save within their own mind, which is the one place that humanity may always enjoy liberty). With liberty, respecting duty, that same prisoner, freed, may create things of beauty or rescue mankind from disease.

## Justice & Mercy

*Justice* and *mercy* are principles forming an inseparable dyad under Truth, with *law* at their intersection. As with *duty* and *liberty*, neither principle can properly exist without the other. Justice requires mercy—discretion in the context of the situation—to be just. Justice without mercy becomes increasingly punitive, seeking ever more "perfect" justice for increasingly minute transgressions, until justice in truth has been supplanted by ruthless retribution for contrived transgressions incomprehensible to the transgressor. Therefore, justice reigns when mercy abounds. Yet an overabundance of mercy without the appropriate measure of justice results in anarchy, stymieing the ability to provide justice. But given justice and mercy, justice is tempered with respect to both the situation and the transgressor, yielding the correct balance to rightly address the transgression and satisfy those wronged.

## Justice

*Justice* is derived directly from *wisdom* as the right application of truth in light of a transgression, typically as a breach of law or duty. *Justness* is the Truth Behavior recognizing the principles of *justice* and *mercy*.

While duty counters personal licentiousness, justice counters unchecked licentiousness within a society. Justice is a state of correctness under Truth, not a base of power from which to mete out correction, although this difference would be indistinguishable if it were possible for fallible humanity to perfect impartial distribution of justice. Justice only occurs at the individual level and is not a respecter of persons—it must apply equally to all without regard for position, wealth, age, or any other characteristic. Proper justice is restorative to those who are redeemable in society and repentant of their transgression.

Justice cannot be divided. Providing "justice" to someone at the expense of injustice to another is not practicing justice. Such is only a shift in favor, and justice permits no favoritism. This is why Justice is often depicted as a blindfolded woman holding a balance scale, connoting appropriate measure of justice for the transgression, and a sword, connoting proper authority for the administration of that justice.

"Group justice" always creates injustice for someone, which is why "social justice"—which contends that it effects justice for a selected class of people by applying "corrective" biases or preferences to the general administration of justice—is not justice. Such attempts to "adjust" justice are why vast punitive measures against a group or class of people (like the punishing terms of the World War I Treaty of Versailles on Germany) often leads to further conflict. Seldom are all people in some group equally guilty, and some are not at all guilty (the young), and the injustice they experience in wrongly applied "retributive" or "corrective" justice leads some of them to seek redress or revenge through further conflict.

## Corrupting Core Principles

Beware of qualifications to timeless principles. Qualifiers modify the principle, limiting or altering its meaning, often corrupting, even directly countering, the base principle. Consider "social justice" and "environmental justice." Because these two popular movements conflict in many situations, neither can fully deliver justice. Other examples include "my" truth, "social" democracy, and "stakeholder" capitalism.

## Justice vs. Fairness

Fairness is not the same as justice. Justice is an objective requirement of Truth. Fairness is subjective, determined by the consent of involved parties. Consider a teacher interrupting a children's game at recess to change their rules of play. Without a say in the process or without explanation of how the new rules are just, the children will never agree to their fairness. But a group of children on a playground agreeing to their own rules for a game implicitly deem the rules fair. If they did not, they would simply take their ball and go home.

## Mercy

*Mercy* is derived from *love* and seeks redemption for a transgressor. Mercy provides a remittance for all or part of the penalty of justice.

Frequently tied to contrition by the transgressor, mercy is often delivered by formal authority rather than the party actually offended by the transgression. Mercy counts the cost of the transgression, its impact on all parties, and accounts for the whole of the circumstance in justice, choosing to address the transgression as if it had not occurred or had occurred to a lesser degree. However, mercy does not require forgiveness and does not forget the transgression for which mercy was given. For example, a convicted drunk driver may have their license suspended and receive community service for a first offense where the just penalty requires jail time. But if there is another offense, the first offense may be considered, and a harsher penalty given.

Clemency is similar to, but different from, mercy. Clemency is mercy granted for purely practical or political reasons, not directly for the sake of the offended or the transgressor. For instance, clemency is demonstrated in the release of a prisoner in order to keep the public peace or because there is no jail space. Guilty convicts plead for clemency in sentencing rather than mercy because they are undeserving of mercy. This distinction between clemency and mercy is important to separate the natural order principle of mercy from pragmatic action that does not conform to principle.

## Law

At the intersection of *justice* and *mercy* properly resides *law*. When the proper response in truth is undiscernible in the spiritual order, law substitutes in the natural order to set a standard of justice with balance in mercy. Because law is a substitute for right response discerned in truth, law may, in practice, be humane or inhumane, good or wicked. Wicked law without truth and mercy becomes a tool for tyranny. Humane law must comport with truth and provide justice while also providing for circumstances to be considered in the administration of justice, including the opportunity for mercy. For example, Law recognizes that murder is a transgression of law, but that homicide in self-defense is not a transgression of law, despite the same outcome—death inflicted on one person by another. Similarly, a murder by one found to be of unfit mind is counted as transgression of law, but mercy is provided to the transgressor by commuting a punitive sentence to one of incarceration for mental care.

Sir William Blackstone understood that humane law must comport with truth in respect to a higher authority when he wrote *An Analysis of the Laws of England*. In it, he expressed the basis for English law, which was also used as the blueprint for law in America's founding. Blackstone's summary of how law should be created and interpreted parallels the process of discerning truth in reason, conscience, intuition, and inspiration, leading to law with appropriate balance of justice and mercy.

> ### Blackstone's Nature of Laws
>
> LAW is a Rule of Action, prescribed by a superior Power.
>
> Natural Law is the Rule of human Action, prescribed by the Creator, and discoverable by the Light of Reason.
>
> The divine, or revealed, Law (considered as a Rule of Action) is also the Law of Nature, imparted by God himself.
>
> Society is formed for the Protection of Individuals; and States, or Government, for the Preservation of Society.
>
> To interpret a Law, we must enquire after the Will of the Maker: Which may be collected either from the Words, the Context, the Subject-matter, the Effects and Consequence, or the Spirit and Reason of the Law.
>
> From the latter Method of Interpretation [the Spirit and Reason of the Law] arises Equity, or the Correction of that wherein the Law (by reason of its Universality) is deficient (18) (abridged).

## Equality

*Equality* is the principle proclaiming that each person in all of humanity is created equal in value. *Equality* is a principle of Truth, deriving from *duty* and *justice* apart from the influence of *liberty* and *mercy*. This is because it is right (just) and required (duty) to treat others equally without the choice (liberty) to excuse (mercy) the practice of inequality. While talent, intelligence, beauty, and other individual human characteristics are distributed unequally across all of humanity, equality in value is uniform among all people. The implication is that all life has value because if a person believes that they have inherent value or believes that any other person has inherent value, then, being equal, all people have inherent value, worthy of respect. Therefore, the Truth Behavior of the principle of *equality* is *respect for life*.

# Spiritual Order Principles of Truth

The Spiritual Order Principles of Truth, activated via *love* and *wisdom*, are *gratitude* and *virtue*. *Gratitude* and *virtue* are spiritual principles because they function beyond natural impetus, only relating to humankind—baby chicks are never grateful, and the industriousness of ants is not virtuous despite its communal benefit.

## Gratitude

*Gratitude* is personal awareness of material sacrifice or advocacy received, comprehending its value with sincere heartfelt appreciation. *Gratitude* is based in *love* and *wisdom,* and its practice leads to the Truth Behaviors *compassion*, *contentment*, *discipline*, *forgiveness*, and *humility*.

Gratitude requires the recognition that one cannot live to the fullest without truth and positive support while wisdom tempers the potential for confusing gratitude with a fearful, weak, and needy reliance on continuing affirmation. Without gratitude, one is more likely to become prideful, believing that they alone established their circumstances. Upon close examination, this is never the case. There is always another level of reflection possible that reveals reliance on, or assistance from, others, even if it is just from the sacrifices and creativity of others produced throughout time.

Gratitude is often used synonymously with thankfulness, but thankfulness is approval of a person or thing in a circumstance, whereas gratitude is appreciation persisting beyond the situation. And one can be grateful without being thankful. For example, someone raised by awful, even cruel, parents may not be thankful for those parents who caused them pain and suffering but may be grateful to those same parents for giving them life and ensuring their survival. One can be thankful for anything for which they have gratitude, but thankfulness alone can still leave room for pride and selfishness—an athlete may be thankful that they won first prize but not have gratitude to parents, coaches, or others who helped with the achievement.

There is a difference between the phrasing, *gratitude to* and *gratitude for*. One can say they are *grateful for* anything. "I'm grateful for sunny days." "I'm grateful for this forest of trees." These are not expressions of gratitude. They are, at best, statements of personal admiration, and they are insipid platitudes at worst,

## Spiritual Order Principles of Truth 65

ignoring reality in vacant Pollyannaism rather than demonstration of gratitude in truth. On the other hand, to be *grateful to* a forest of trees or to a generic cosmos for one's life or circumstances (like the ancient Athenian altar of worship which was inscribed, "To the unknown god"), and deeming it as being spiritual gratitude is simply a guise for false humility. Whether consciously or not, such a declaration is a justification for self-praise, effectively saying, "I am grateful to random circumstances," which really implies the belief, "I made this happen, but I offer credit elsewhere to demonstrate my [false] humility." Certainly, one can say they are *thankful* for a forest of trees—for shade, for wood, or for beauty—but gratitude must be given *to* a participatory outside source of provision, such as parents, a mentor, ancestors, past leaders, or God.

The gratitude-driven behaviors are practiced, for benefit of self and others, in appreciation of the past actions and sacrifices of others. They are driven by gratitude with the understanding that "It's not all about me," even in cases where there is much room to claim personal accomplishment. This understanding goes beyond exercises of duty or justice or equality in the natural order because gratitude involves human reflection or conscience or other spiritual understanding. So, when it is said that *humility* is a practice derived from *gratitude*, it means that humility comes from appreciating that one's life, place in life, capabilities, etc., are enabled in the sacrifices and actions of others.

> ## Pollyannaism
>
> Pollyannaism is the trait of having an overly optimistic or irrationally positive outlook in all aspects of life, typically exhibiting inordinate cheerfulness or exuberance. Pollyannaism is named for the title character, Pollyanna, of a 1913 novel and 1960 motion picture, who displayed such characteristics. While the outward expression of Pollyannaism appears as being joyful, and the practice of seeking good in all things is commendable, Pollyannaism implies irrationality and self-deception in dealing with hardship, which can lead to negative consequences.

## Virtue

*Virtue* is the outward expression of internalized behaviors derived from *wisdom* and *love*. The key Truth Behaviors comprising *virtue* are *altruism, courage, forbearance, gentleness, honesty, kindness, long-suffering,* and *self-control*.

Virtue, simplified, is the choice for personal betterment on the side of good, in the continuous practice of the Golden Rule. As such, virtuous behavior cannot be undergirded with foolishness, ignorance, or wickedness.

Suppose someone rushes into a burning home and, by opening the door and rushing through the house, rouses the family from sleep, enabling them to escape the fire. This would be a virtuous act only if its intent were to rescue the family. If the intent were to escape the police after committing a robbery and rousing the family accidental, there would be no virtue in the action.

Virtue is often viewed as a catch-all term for superlative good behavior, seemingly unobtainable by all but the most heroic and perfect of character. The good news is that virtue is open to all who choose to act in wisdom and love. However, every valiant or pleasing act is not necessarily virtue. Virtue does not include behaviors that can readily be exercised in wickedness as well as for good, such as loyalty. Virtue also does not include the collection of behaviors that may be honored or simply appreciated by others, unless providing significant betterment or benefit to others. For example, wittiness may be a positive behavior and well-liked in conversation, but it is not a virtue because it provides no value beyond immediate engagement and entertainment.

## Gratitude & Virtue

While all principles of Truth interact and support each other, *gratitude* and *virtue,* in combination, produce yet more right behaviors—*excellence*, *generosity*, *goodness,* and *steadfastness*. These behaviors bear the signs of virtues evident outside of oneself, but are ad hoc in expression and so require the internality of gratitude to be sustained and ingrained in life.

> ## Honor
>
> Honor received is different from virtue achieved. The word, "honorable" literally means "able to be honored" or "worthy of honor." This is a clear indication that honor is externally bestowed, unlike virtue which is developed internally and expressed outwardly. However, in everyday usage, virtue is often equated to honor as *honorability*, much as the American founders stated in the Declaration of Independence, "we mutually pledge to each other our Lives, our Fortunes, and our sacred Honor (7)," to say that they gave up all claims of virtue should they renege on their commitment to independence.
>
> All things which may be honored may not be virtuous. Honor can be misapplied or even falsely ascribed. An evil dictator may be honored by his people while his wicked conduct and pride demonstrate that he is devoid of virtue.

# Truth-Based Learning Framework

The Truth Principles and Truth Behaviors that have been discussed self-organize into a visual framework showing their relationships. This Truth-Based Learning Framework shown in the diagram on page 72 is a refinement of the high-level diagram from page 34. *Truth* is at the center, with the *Operating Principles of Truth—Love* and *Wisdom* (with *Discernment*)—above and below it. *Love* is an internal principle, being chiefly a measure of one's "heart," which represents the essence of one's beliefs and thoughts. *Wisdom* is an external principle, outwardly directing the right application of truth.

To the left side of *Truth*, *Love*, and *Wisdom* lie the *Natural Order Principles of Truth*—those principles required for people to live together in family and society. To the right side lie the *Spiritual Order Principles of Truth*, those required for civilization beyond society. To the outside of the principles on both sides are their *Truth Behaviors* which, when learned and practiced, enable individual betterment and promote human flourishing.

The *Natural Order* (left) side of the framework includes the principle dyads, *Liberty-Duty* and *Justice-Mercy*. From *Liberty-Duty* derives the behavior, *Dutifulness*, and from *Justice-Mercy,* the derived behavior is *Justness*. Each dyad forms a Venn diagram with the intersection being the collective societal consequence of the intersecting principles. The intersection of *Liberty-Duty* is *Culture*, and the intersection of *Justice-Mercy* is *Law*. Culture and law, together, define the natural order "tools" available to build—or to destroy—society.

The *Liberty-Duty* and *Justice-Mercy* dyads of the *Natural Order* framework also enable the principle of *Equality*, which drives *Respect for Life*. And connected only to *Liberty* are the elements *Personality*, an input to *Liberty*, and *Creativity*, an output of *Liberty*. These elements of individual liberty provide a conduit for Spiritual Order Truth Behaviors to "leak" into the Natural Order through individual action and, in aggregate, have the potential to strongly move popular culture in one direction or another.

The *Spiritual Order* (right) side of the framework includes the principles *Gratitude* and *Virtue*. *Gratitude* generates the behaviors *Compassion*, *Contentment*, *Discipline*, *Forgiveness*, and *Humility*. *Virtue* produces the behaviors *Altruism*, *Courage*, *Forbearance*, *Gentleness*, *Honesty*, *Kindness*, *Long-Suffering,* and *Self-Control*. In combination, *Gratitude* and *Virtue* produce more right behaviors, *Excellence*, *Generosity, Goodness*, and *Steadfastness*.

> ## Internal & External Principles
>
> Understanding the principles of Truth may be aided by aligning each as being an *internal* principle or an *external* principle. Internal principles chiefly relate to one's internal well-being and growth while external principles more directly pertain to interactions with others. The framework "axis" on which internal and external principles ride runs across the *Natural* and *Spiritual Orders* so that there are both internal and external principles for each. Internal behaviors tend to be based in *Liberty*, *Duty,* and *Gratitude*, whereas external principles chiefly flow from *Virtue*, *Justice,* and *Mercy*, but there is no hard line of separation across internal and external principles—internal principles do apply to external relationships, and exercise of external principles necessarily has internal effects.

72 TRUTH-BASED LEARNING

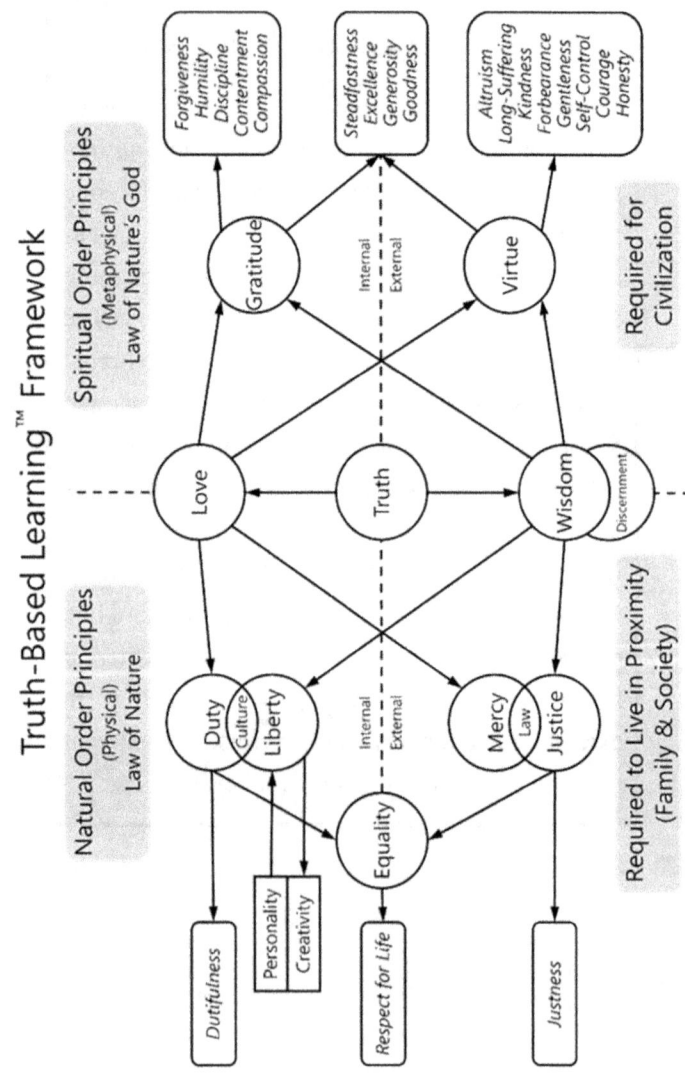

# Truth Practices Flow

The Truth-Based Learning Framework relates the principles of Truth to the behaviors that embody those principles, but it does not provide sufficient organization to easily turn those behaviors into actionable practices for personal betterment. The Truth Practices Flow diagram (page 76) organizes the behaviors into practice groups, each with a common purpose, to make learning the behaviors practical and to simplify regular reflection in areas needed for personal development.

The Truth Practices Flow may be leveraged step by step as a guide for learners, repeating the process in deepening levels of study over time, or as a gauge to analyze popular culture and current events as opportunities arise. For mature and experienced learners, the Truth Practices Flow may be used as a checklist for self-examination, or for delving into each purpose and practice in search of undiscovered truth.

The arrow flowing from left to right in the diagram signifies the process of moving forward in learning and personal betterment. Within the arrow, the purposes for personal betterment are staged, and below each purpose, the Truth Practices that support that purpose are listed. For example, the practices *Respect for Life*, *Justness,* and *Dutifulness* are grouped to support the purpose *Live as a Citizen*. The purposes are ordered within the arrow suggesting that the more fundamental purposes and practices should be learned before tackling the more mature purposes and practices—*Live as a Citizen* should be addressed before there is an expectation of being able to *Flourish*.

However, the flow does not imply that "early" practices are strict prerequisites of "later" practices because there is no "certificate of completion" for any practice—they are all lifelong learning efforts with deeper understanding and achievement always possible.

The Truth Practices Flow diagram also shows that several of the purposes can themselves be aggregated into summary purposes. The purposes *Choose Betterment*, *Find Right Sense of Self*, and *Resolve to Defend Truth* are all introspective purposes leading one to *Examine Self*. Similarly, the purposes *Hone Relationships*, *Value Others,* and *Sacrifice for Others* all lead one to *Appreciate Others*.

When grouped at the top (summary) level of purposes, the Truth Practices Flow is easy to recall: *Live as a Citizen, Examine Self, Appreciate Others, Flourish.* This progression should appear familiar. The Truth Practices Flow aligns with the goals of learning—living well in liberty according to one's desires and capabilities, striving for betterment, respecting the rights of others to do the same, and building relationships, resulting in a flourishing human civilization.

With the Truth-Based Learning Framework and Truth Practices Flow in mind, each of the Truth Practices, grouped by purpose, may be examined for the facilitation of personal betterment.

# Truth-Based Learning™ Truth Practices Flow™

| Live as a Citizen | Examine Self | | | Appreciate Others | | | Flourish |
|---|---|---|---|---|---|---|---|
| | Choose Betterment | Find Right Sense of Self | Resolve to Defend Truth | Hone Relationships | Value Others | Sacrifice for Others | |
| Respect for Life | Self-Control | Contentment | Honesty | Long-Suffering | Compassion | Altruism | Goodness |
| Justness | Discipline | Humility | Courage | Forbearance | Gentleness | Generosity | Excellence |
| Dutifulness | | Forgiveness | | Steadfastness | Kindness | | |

# Personal Betterment

Truth Behaviors may be taught but cannot be indoctrinated. They can only be ingrained through individual willingness to learn and practice them. Personal betterment—a goal of learning—begins with that intentional choice. But the *intention* of developing behaviors, without actually doing it, yields nothing but self-deception. There is no value in academic learning just to treat the principles of Truth as unactioned philosophy. Seekers of truth must be doers and not just hearers of truth. Only when practiced and preserved do the behaviors of Truth provide value—personal betterment and support for human flourishing.

The collection and outward expression of a person's behaviors, good or bad, are what is called one's *character*. Truth being eternal and good, the behaviors derived from the principles of Truth generate positive traits counter to foolishness and wickedness. This regular exhibition of the good behaviors of Truth is called *good character*, or *personal integrity*. Because truth is eternal and good and because character reflects one's heart more so than one's doctrine, the practices of Truth, and its defense, are of value to everyone whether religious, agnostic, or atheist—only the decidedly wicked might disagree with the value of any Truth Practice.

Using the Truth Practices Flow for structure, each purpose and practice of Truth is reviewed in this chapter, ordered by purpose group.

## Purpose – Live as a Citizen

The first-stage purpose of the Truth Practices Flow is to live as a citizen, a peaceful, law-abiding, dutiful—and free—member of society. The practices of *respect for life*, *dutifulness*, and *justness* are grouped here because, being part of the natural order, they are the minimum practices for living peaceably and productively in society, which sets the stage for personal betterment.

### *Practice – Respect for Life*

Respect for human life is an outward-facing behavior which derives from the principle of *equality*, coming from combined *duty* and *justice*. *Respect for life* is listed first in the Truth Practices, before *dutifulness* and *justness*, despite its longer derivation from Truth because respect for life is incredibly important for developing fundamental human relationships and for establishing and sustaining the other Truth Practices.

All life has inherent value—life is to be respected for the benefit of the individual being respected, the benefit of the individual giving respect, and society. Without respect for life, authoritarianism—by mob, warlord, junta, or dictator—will take hold as truth succumbs to lust for power and control, and liberty dies as vengeance replaces justice and mercy.

Respect for life should not show favoritism, all people being equal in value. In reality, people have biases for family, friends, those who share common interests, countrymen, and more. These biases tend to be personal affinities toward some, more so than negative biases against others, but there should be no bias in favor of one person over another in extending natural and spiritual good.

Respect for life does not require respect for others' actions, attitudes, or beliefs. Acknowledging the inherent worth of another person is not the same as agreeing with everything they say or do. Respect for life does include respect for others' property because property represents one's ability to survive and succeed. This is also why it is wrong to steal or to crave someone else's property. These actions put self above others and, worse, put one in contention with others.

Respect for life comprehends that it is wrong to murder, but also recognizes that killing in self-defense is not murder. Of course, there is a difference between a sanction to take a life in self-defense and a desire to do so. One may even choose not to exercise self-defense, instead opting for self-sacrifice in respect for the life of another (19).

The principle of equality is directly assaulted when respect for life is diminished. When the taking of life—via abortion, euthanasia, eugenics, indiscriminate self-defense, even excessive use of the death penalty for justice—is casual and pervasive in a culture, equality diminishes. This is because there is always one more reason to take (or diminish) life, and wickedness is always seeking to leverage the taking of life to gain power.

*Respect for life* is more than just a rote practice of Truth, and is much more than the celebration of individual differences commonly called "diversity." Respecting life based on "diversity" often leads down a path to contempt for life demanded by the party spirit embodied in the celebration of differences—celebrating the lives of one group tends to diminish the value of the lives of other groups. Instead, respect for life must be a foundation of personal belief, the first thought about another person's inherent worth conceived in love, confirmed through wisdom, and aligned with eternal truth. When it is not, one must pause in introspection, examine themselves for prejudices and unfair bias, and *decide* to respect the life of every person. To choose otherwise ultimately derails any other attempt to practice truth for personal betterment and human flourishing.

## *Practice – Dutifulness*

*Dutifulness* as a Truth Practice encompasses that natural, instinctive duty—based in *storge* love and exercised with individual liberty—that is informed and uncoerced in relationship to others.

Dutifulness is often equated with responsibility, but responsibility can also mean culpability for wrongdoing or coerced obligation. Similarly, conscientiousness seems to equate to duty, but it stands in the spiritual order, including duty-like actions driven by conscience but not necessarily required by duty. Conscientiousness may also be deemed "doing what needs to be done" irrespective of importance—it may be conscientious to mow the lawn each week, but there is no natural duty to do so.

To practice *dutifulness* requires recognition of appropriate duties. This may be simple in some cases—a parent with children has a duty to care for them—or it may be more challenging to gauge. Is it a duty to help a person found injured along a road, or is that action optional subject to spiritual behaviors like compassion? Practicing *dutifulness* means asking such questions of oneself in everyday life and erring on the side of right duty and supporting civil duty, while guarding against unjust coercive duty and wrong application of loyalty. The simplest way to gauge right duty is to revisit where it resides in the natural order. Duty is the counter to licentiousness in liberty and drives the natural obligation in respect for life. Therefore, consideration for the rights and value of others drives duty and empowers justice and mercy.

## *Practice – Justness*

*Justness* is an outward-facing practice, focused on acting in, and standing for, justice in all situations, even when it runs contrary to personal comfort or benefit. In addition to supporting right justice, justness can also easily be characterized by its constituent behaviors, including impartiality, objectivity, mercy, rejection of faction, and active opposition to injustice.

Practicing justness may be most effective by discerning injustice because the presence of injustice gnaws at a justice seeker, while justice served often goes unnoticed because it is right—people seldom take notice of good health, but they notice when they are sick. Injustice may be known by studying liberty and rights, understanding the balance of one person's rights with those of another, and discerning where liberty ends and licentiousness begins. Additionally, to discern injustice in society one must understand what constitutes just law based in truth—as opposed to capricious law based in the fleeting nature of pop culture—and ensure that just law is applied equally.

## Purpose – Choose Betterment

One must make a personal choice to move beyond just living as a citizen in society to becoming a better person for the benefit of oneself and others. Others can help support betterment but cannot force it nor confer it. Fortunately, no special talent is required, just a desire to learn and become better. This starts with the practices of *self-control* and *discipline,* which provide direction and endurance for that choice.

## *Practice – Self-Control*

*Self-control* is the exercise of one's personal will—willpower—to manage one's own desires, emotions, and inclinations. It is the start of self-betterment. Self-control enables one to manage those areas of one's life which need either advancement or moderation, both the areas that are completely personal and those affecting relationships with others. For example, unchecked gluttony—lack of self-control in eating—leads to poor personal health in obesity, possibly injures finances, and may adversely affect opportunities to develop relationships.

*Self-control* as a practice of *virtue* runs internal checks in everyday situations to counter tendencies toward foolish and wicked behaviors like laziness, debauchery, indecent behavior, covetousness, jealousy, pride, and selfish ambition. Self-control is also a key enabler of other virtuous behaviors—forbearance, long-suffering, and gentleness—and provides a restraint for the avoidance of licentiousness while employing liberty.

Self-control is not a one-and-done, lasting virtue across all situations, but rather is a conscious decision for betterment in each given situation. One may exhibit great self-control in not getting drunk on Friday night but then get drunk on Saturday. Self-control is required in each incident and past self-control does not ensure present self-control. That said, practicing self-control in any applicable situation provides confidence and experience for practicing self-control in future situations, which can lead to the development of discipline.

## *Practice – Discipline*

*Discipline* is a practice of intentional, motivated repetition to achieve a standard or goal. It is at the core of all Truth Behaviors because it helps to sustain each of them as Truth Practices.

Gratitude motivates discipline through the inherent recognition that the sacrifice necessary to be disciplined is only possible in appreciation of the sacrifices and actions of others, propelling the desire to do better for oneself and others. Discipline is initiated by strength of will—an act of self-control—driven through desire for achievement. Therefore, discipline is practiced out of personal desire and gratitude, spurred by self-control, like an athlete wanting to be the best because they enjoy the sport and are driven by gratitude for their ability and opportunity.

Discipline differs from self-control in persistence. Self-control is an anecdotal action, whereas discipline is repetitive and persistent action. An athlete requires discipline to train and succeed over the long term, and self-control to avoid eating an unhealthy fast-food meal before a big game. Both are necessary to strive for betterment.

Setbacks in discipline may happen but acknowledgement of the failure may improve future discipline by accentuating the gratitude that first enabled it. Discipline is also greatly aided by having someone provide accountability in the effort—another source for gratitude—as exemplified in the sponsorship role in the Twelve Steps recovery process of Alcoholics Anonymous (20).

Through discipline, behaviors are sustained and tend to become habits. Habits, in turn, take over in the times one lacks motivation for conscious discipline. Then, recognizing that the habit ultimately fades to subpar rote behavior, discipline resurfaces through another conscious act of self-control.

*Discipline* is also used as a term for the imposition of compulsory (sometimes punitive) tasks by an authority. Reasonable compulsory discipline is exemplified by military discipline in everything from making one's bed to wearing a proper uniform and maintaining a strict hierarchy of authority. While compulsory discipline is not the target of Truth-Based Learning, many people find gratitude in the experience and choose to continue the discipline when they are no longer under authority. This also exemplifies the purpose for teaching children basic life skills like brushing their teeth. However, whether enforced in childhood or not, discipline in all areas—relationships, finances, health, etc.—must be personally developed for contentment and virtuous culture.

> ### Habit Is Not the Goal
>
> Habit is the result of discipline that one falls back on when one's motivation fails. Habit is mindless rote repetition, ingrained in one's behavior, and may be either good or bad. While habit associated with positive behaviors is good, its effect degrades in time without added motivation or intention. Therefore, habit is not the goal, just the backstop to prevent failure in reaching the goal until discipline can be reestablished.
>
> The classic book *The 7 Habits of Highly Effective People* (21) by Stephen R. Covey, is aptly titled to convey its self-help purpose, but perhaps should have been called "*The 7 Disciplines...*"—there is no habit for "seek first to understand, then to be understood." That requires discipline!

## Purpose – Find Right Sense of Self

With the decision made, and practices begun, for self-betterment, the right sense of self for betterment must be established in truth through *contentment*, *forgiveness*, and *humility*. These practices all stem from *gratitude* because of the introspection required to live with others in peace, live gratefully, and become better.

### *Practice – Contentment*

Contentment is the state of being satisfied, in particular being satisfied even when the situation or circumstances may be less than pleasing. Contentment is the product of peace, joy, and hope, which can only be lasting in gratitude.

Peace, personal peace, is one's resolute acceptance of a situation, whether good or bad, without fear, hatred, anger, or contempt. Peace enables one to emotionally rest in the prevailing conditions (but does not mean a person cannot react to the situation). Joy—delight or satisfaction with gratitude—enables one to respond positively to conditions, understanding that despite a potentially poor outcome at the moment, one's overall circumstance is tenable. Hope—grateful optimism—assuages any glimmers of doubt remaining in joy and peace, filling any gaps in one's ability to fully accept peace and joy with expectation for an improved situation. Together, peace, joy, and hope compound their individual effects to establish a behavior greater than any one sentiment alone.

In this, contentment permits satisfaction in tough times, allows for consideration of others' needs, enables the pursuit of higher goals by not leaving one stuck in dissatisfaction, and activates a rational expectation for the future.

Contentment does not imply complacency. Complacency is self-satisfied contentment—laziness—or apathetic, unprepared indifference when faced with an impending challenge. Complacency lacks gratitude, rejecting with contempt the value or opportunity in a situation.

Industriousness and the desire for personal growth and to exercise one's talents are part of human nature and should not be forsaken by mistaking complacency for contentment. For example, one may be content with their financial situation but still seek a higher-paying job because they enjoy the challenge. In contrast, complacency is exemplified by the biblical proverb, "The lazy one buries his hand in the dish, but will not even bring it back to his mouth" (19:24).

## *Practice – Forgiveness*

Just as gratitude is a personal choice, so is forgiveness. Forgiveness freely and purposefully does not count the cost of a transgression. Forgiveness chooses to ignore and expunge the transgression as if it had not occurred—permanently. This is not to say that one must actually forget the transgression to provide forgiveness, but it does mean that the one forgiving gives up all resentment, offense, and future claims on leveraging the transgression for gain.

Forgiveness has the internal benefit of providing peace to the forgiver in the matter. In forgiving, the forgiver gives up anger and offense at the other party as a function of their gratitude to those whose forgiveness or favor they have received. Externally, forgiveness offers the same peace to the offending party. It frees them, if they so choose, to move on without building up hatred or desire for revenge, and enables new relationship. In aggregate, forgiveness promotes a society of peace and relationship.

The gratitude found in being forgiven enables forgiveness of others. But forgiveness is not a reciprocal transaction of "I'll forgive you if you forgive me." Such transactional "forgiveness" is not heartfelt nor driven by gratitude and is unlikely to last.

*Forgiveness* is an individual practice for the restoration of relationship and well-being, not a societal practice. Forgiveness is not the same as mercy or clemency, and forgiveness does not remit responsibility for actions nor forsake justice and law.

*Forgiveness* as a practice tends to be punctuated by noteworthy events, which challenge one to reach deep into their desire to be at peace with themselves and others and to forgive when they have been truly affronted. But forgiveness should also be a daily practice of overlooking small insults—ignoring being cut off in traffic—and being empathetic to others, not being offended by someone else's bad mood or angry response and therefore not even needing to forgive.

## *Practice – Humility*

Humility is one of the most counterfeited and manipulated human behaviors because it is one of the most difficult to achieve in practice. This is especially so when one has had success in athletics, scholarship, or other practices like generosity. These, if separated from gratitude, love, and wisdom, tempt one to pride, limiting personal betterment and destroying relationships. The true benefit of humility is the end of pride.

Humility in gratitude recognizes that whatever excellence or generosity or goodness one possesses, it was achieved with the support or effort of others, even if that effort is far removed in time, built into the foundation of civilization. This is not to say that humility denies credit for individual excellence or generosity. Humility actually demands pursuit of excellence to avoid humility being overcome by apathy or abandoned to the pursuit of vices.

Humility does, however, require that credit is not the inordinate goal of one's actions, especially for actions which are intended to benefit others. An athlete in a competition seeks excellence and reasonably desires the accolades that come with achievement. That athlete can relish the achievement in humility or in its opposite, hubris. In humility, the athlete accepts and enjoys the accolades and moves on to the next goal. In hubris, the athlete enjoys the accolade more than it is intended, lives in the past achievement, and diminishes the achievements of others in self-aggrandizement of the achievement. Hubris often feigns humility with words or actions, thereby seeking even more accolades for being both humble and excellent.

With the recognition that humility can be so easily faked, one of the best ways to begin the practice of *humility* is to act it out even if elements of pride remain in one's mind. The challenge, then, is to reflect on the humility professed and the pride felt, and to find the flaws in the pride—to identify those elements that required the support of others, or which were purely matters of circumstance—and then to direct that understanding into the practice of *humility* until the recognition of the requirement for personal gratitude becomes internalized above the selfish need to express pride.

## Purpose – Resolve to Defend Truth

Given a right sense of self and resolve to better oneself, that resolve must be extended to the defense of truth. Without defense, truth may be overwhelmed by falsehood—lies—limiting liberty and individual betterment and stunting civilization. While confined in a Soviet Russian gulag, dissident Aleksandr Solzhenitsyn authored the essay "Live not by Lies," in which he provided ample firsthand rationale for the basic defense of truth under an authoritarian regime, pronouncing,

> [T]he simplest, the most accessible key to our liberation: *a personal nonparticipation in lies!* Even if all is covered by lies, even if all is under their rule, let us resist in the smallest way: Let their rule hold *not through me!*... For when people renounce lies, lies simply cease to exist. (22)

Truth is defended by, and tyranny ultimately overcome through, non-participation in lies, which is effected through the Truth Practices, *honesty* and *courage*. Honesty in oneself, and requiring it in others, is the defense against lies. Practicing honesty takes courage. Without courage, it is not easy to question someone's truthfulness or to call out bald-faced lies. Without courage, one will lie rather than deal with the consequences of truth.

Defense of truth is a burden. There are always attacks against even the most commonplace truths from the people who defend foolishness, ignorance, and wickedness. But honesty and courage strengthen one to live in truth, even with failure, and in the face of external adversity. There is nothing in Truth-Based Learning that will stop untruth from corrupting the principles and practices of Truth unless people wield the truth and build a culture of truth, not just as the norm, but as the highest aspiration in society.

## Pride and Offense

Pride is excessive self-esteem or pleasure in oneself, or self-gratification in the deeds of someone else.

Pride causes one to stumble in the face of offense. There is always someone better than you at any given thing, or there will be. There will always be others who will rate you differently than you think you should be rated. There are always people who will be jealous of you or hate you if you are indeed excellent. In pride, you will be offended at each of these people, leading you to seek to defend your pride or disparage your accuser. As the biblical proverb says, "Pride goes before destruction, and a haughty spirit before stumbling" (16:18).

The Greek word for offense is *skandalon* (23), which translates to "bait stick," the trigger of a trap to which the bait is tied. Offense is a trap and so is the pride that leads to it.

The behaviors of Truth hold the answer to avoiding pride. Joy and gratitude are the proper outlet for satisfaction in one's own excellence, not pride. Admiration, blessing, thankfulness, or joy is the proper response to the excellence of others, not pride.

## *Practice – Honesty*

*Honesty* is the virtue of continually acting in truth. To practice honesty, speak the truth. Be clear in what is known, what is surmised, and what is theorized—exaggeration easily shifts to lying. Practicing honesty sustains truth and sheds light on foolishness and wickedness. Practicing honesty also grows self-awareness and drives introspection, which furthers the practice of other Truth Behaviors. If one cannot be honest with oneself, one cannot successfully practice truth in other areas. Practicing honesty does not require interacting with others in a blunt or unkind manner. Gentleness and forbearance benefit the practice of *honesty* when dealing with truth that may grieve others, tempering its delivery without breaching truthfulness.

The opposite of honesty is dishonesty—lying—which is explicitly, or by omission, not acting in truth. Lying one time tends to lead to new lies to cover for the old lies, the multitude of lies breeding foolishness and the growing frequency of lies becoming wickedness.

## *Practice – Courage*

*Courage* is the unwavering ability to face adversity. Courage is a practice rather than a status to be achieved. One may *act courageously*, at any given moment showing bravery or heroism, but continuous courage requires practice borne of self-control and aided by discipline. However, no one is always courageous or heroic, and courage may fail, but courage includes the ability to face new adversity in light of, and despite, past failure.

The practice of *courage* is valuable to thwart fear and inaction, which are the tools of foolishness, ignorance, and wickedness. Fear crushes the practices of the principles of Truth, leading one to capitulate with wickedness, tacitly, if not actively. Even when unafraid, lack of courage to act in truth—apathy—hinders the defense of truth and ultimately leads to subjugation by untruth.

## Purpose – Hone Relationships

With the introspective Truth Practices that bring right sense of self and lead to defense of truth understood, attention can be turned to honing relationships with (other) imperfect humans to reduce potential friction and to better appreciate others' perspectives, while at the same time developing greater satisfaction in those relationships. The Truth Practices for honing relationships are *long-suffering*, *forbearance*, and *steadfastness*.

## *Practice – Long-Suffering*

*Long-suffering* is a virtue, a kind of patience adding an element of suffering or exceptional endurance which provides focus and rationale for its continuation. Long-suffering is most often associated with a situational stimulus, with or without personal interaction. For example, one may exhibit long-suffering in living with a physical deformity for which forbearance has no relevance. The United States Declaration of Independence provides another example of the concept of long-suffering:

> Governments long established should not be changed for light and transient causes; and accordingly, all experience hath shewn, that mankind are more disposed to suffer, while evils are sufferable, than to right themselves by abolishing the forms to which they are accustomed. (7)

This means that it is normal and good to suffer for a time, while evils are not too great, rather than to abandon someone or something for "light and transient causes." The Declaration could have been written, "all experience hath shewn that mankind is given to long-suffering, while evils are sufferable…"

Long-suffering is an important practice because the delay in justified action resulting from long-suffering provides time to overcome emotional response, allowing reason and discernment to generate an appropriate course of action. With proper discernment, long-suffering should become more of a temperament than a calculated practice, leaving one always inclined toward long-suffering and allowing discernment to suggest an alternate course of action should the issue require it.

## *Practice – Forbearance*

*Forbearance* is restraint from response to some provocation. Most often relevant in personal interaction, forbearance leverages discretion in reaction and supports patience and forgiveness in just response, restraining the response, at least for a time.

Forbearance is similar to long-suffering, but forbearance implies immediate restraint to an acute provocation while long-suffering exhibits a long-term underlying patience. For example, one can show forbearance as a response to insults from an employer but choose not to be long-suffering in that environment by finding another job.

*Forbearance* can be practiced by practicing *forgiveness* and by checking one's own pride and offense, discerning what affronts are worthy of forbearance and which are threats to truth that must not be tolerated.

## *Practice – Steadfastness*

*Steadfastness* is a firmness of belief in, or resolve for, something or someone, even when standing for that thing is a cause of personal suffering or condemnation.

Gratitude provides the resolve for steadfastness while wisdom ensures virtuous purpose for standing fast in belief. Steadfastness without virtue is just resolute foolishness and without truth is faithful wickedness. Steadfastness cannot long abide untruth or wickedness—the very nature of things untrue guarantees that adherence to an untruth will one day be abandoned for another belief or be forsaken as that untruth morphs into some other untruth.

Firm faithfulness equates to steadfastness. However, faithfulness can be casual where steadfastness is deep-seated. Faithfulness may easily be placed in bad people or wrong principles where steadfastness will not last, and faithfulness tends toward simple adherence to beliefs, whereas steadfastness implies willingness to suffer for beliefs.

Steadfastness in the spiritual order is similar to dutifulness in the natural order, but dutifulness carries an obligation while steadfastness is a voluntary commitment. Steadfastness can also be viewed as the distinguished twin of long-suffering. Long-suffering *puts up with* something in *many* circumstances while steadfastness *stands with something* in *all* circumstances.

Steadfastness has particular importance in Truth-Based Learning—the entire premise of Truth-Based Learning is based on steadfastness in truth. To be righteously steadfast, one must exhibit commitment to truth and courageously defend it. One cannot be considered steadfast in truth while idly standing by as untruth is proclaimed and promulgated.

## Tolerance

Tolerance is different from forbearance or long-suffering.

Tolerance is an allowable deviation from a standard or norm. In terms of relationships, it is indulgence (allowable deviation) of differing beliefs or practices of another (the standard). Tolerance implies some level of acceptance of a deviation, even if not based in truth, whereas forbearance is restraint of action without necessary acceptance while long-suffering chooses suffering over acceptance.

Truth, being eternal and good, is the standard for individual betterment and human flourishing, and deviation from truth results in foolishness, ignorance, and wickedness. Therefore, tolerance cannot be the same as forbearance because tolerance of untruth is wickedness.

## Purpose – Value Others

Where honing relationships with others is largely about learning how to live in acceptance of human imperfection, practicing *compassion, gentleness,* and *kindness* opens the door to truly seeing others as valuable—as more than just another equal being moving through life, as someone important, someone worth engaging and knowing.

Valuing others is the beginning of the admonition to love your neighbor as yourself.

## *Practice – Compassion*

*Compassion* is heartfelt consideration for another person's unfortunate circumstances. *Compassion* is an internal behavior sourced from *gratitude*. It may seem to be an external behavior of *virtue*, but compassion is not just an expression of concern or pity; it includes relating to another's circumstances in sympathy or with empathy, and with selflessness in addressing those circumstances. So, where kindness and gentleness have virtuous effects, and respect for life provides a "kick start" for compassion based in duty and justice, compassion is far more personal and involved in the problems and needs of the other person.

The capacity for compassion is natural but not evenly present across people. Some are simply more sympathetic or empathetic than others, and one's own relatable life experiences increase one's ability to be compassionate toward others in similar circumstances. But compassion can be expanded by practicing love and respect for life without regard to the recipient or their circumstances, and through expression of gratitude for compassion shown to us.

## *Practice – Gentleness*

*Gentleness*, the quality of being gentle, means meeting situations with an even and measured disposition, in duty, with respect for life and liberty—at least with personal consideration, if not with kindness and forbearance.

The approach to practicing *gentleness* can be found in the character of a classic gentleman. A gentleman in society traditionally was a man of his word, reserved, a thoughtful man not rash in thinking or judgment, a man of decorum, able to hold his temper, one giving generously to the needy but not suffering fools—an honorable man. While this notion of a gentleman may have been corrupted to the point of being almost antithetical today, these classic characteristics still apply for one practicing *gentleness*, perhaps with more openness to compassion and gratitude than in the past. Practicing *gentleness* exceeds practicing those individual characteristics to become a temperament with the consequence of treating people like they are not an interruption to one's life.

Gentleness is similar to traditional meekness, which also has changed from its historical meaning. To be meek at one time meant to hold great strength but to temper it with forbearance. Modern usage has left the word neutered, meaning only forbearance—to the point of passivity or cowardice and inability to act. Neither meekness nor gentleness should ever be construed to be cowardice or impotence. The choice not to wield a sword is different from lack of heart in wielding a sword, and checking one's emotional response to the provocations of a fool does not lessen, but rather increases, the good character of the one holding the sword in check.

## Practice – Kindness

*Kindness* is the practice of treating others with care and concern irrespective of their behavior or one's personal feelings about them. Kindness is a calculated choice requiring virtue to practice but not requiring gratitude because it is a more "mechanical" and broader-based practice than *compassion* or *gentleness*. One may exhibit gentleness and still disregard another person due to their behavior or character, but kindness will still find them. At the same time, without gratitude, one is challenged to be able to show kindness because the humility and compassion of gratitude amplifies kindness.

There is a popular phrase, "Practice random acts of kindness," meant to inspire kindness in people. While any kindness has value, intentional kindness, practiced consistently, is of more value to individuals and society than random acts of kindness practiced for dramatic effect.

## Purpose – Sacrifice for Others

The greatest expression of valuing others is in sacrificing for them. Practicing *altruism* and *generosity* develops the basic respect for the value of other people into voluntary sacrifice for other people. Sacrifice in selflessness and love for others is the ultimate blessing in human relationship, a sure sign of personal betterment and the type of purpose which, when plentiful, advances civilization by leaps and bounds.

## *Practice – Altruism*

*Altruism* is selfless consideration or caring for other people, regardless of who they are. Beyond simple kindness, altruism, in practice, is most often expressed in service or generosity. Service is a selfless, virtuous, personally-engaged practice of providing for the physical or emotional needs of others. One may gain satisfaction or honor from providing service or one may benefit through reciprocal action, but the altruistic virtue of performing service only comes through unselfish service for the purpose of blessing someone else rather than for receiving a reward.

*Altruism* is a necessary Truth Practice because virtue, in wisdom, as well as respect for life stemming from understanding of equality, make it clear that caring for others is beneficial to both those in need and the ones helping. This is because altruistic action works at all levels of engagement—meeting individual emergent needs, advancing insufficient individual capabilities, surmounting weaknesses in families, and filling the gaps in social systems—thereby smoothing over the entanglements that tear the fabric of society and confound the pursuit of happiness.

To practice altruism, set aside and schedule time, funds, and resources to serve existing and emergent charitable needs. Leverage kindness as a precursor to *altruism*, making acts of service or provision a natural extension of everyday interactions.

## *Practice – Generosity*

*Generosity* is the selfless, altruistic, giving of one's time, talent, or treasure (property) to others, *in abundance*. And, through *grace*, generosity endows unmerited favor beyond things material. Generosity embodies the call to treat others as better than oneself. It implies going beyond simple service (such as giving one's time) or the provision of trivial need.

*Generosity* as a Truth Behavior focuses on the "heart" behind the act or gift rather than its magnitude in societal terms. Gratitude for what one has been given, and what one is able to share with others, promotes giving in abundance "from the heart." Material abundance is not required to be generous. This is why *generosity* is driven by both *virtue* and *gratitude*, whereas *altruism* is *virtue* driven. More so, the quality of generosity relates to the level of sacrifice in the giving, making the abundance of the poorer giver more generous than a larger but less sacrificial gift of the wealthy giver—a poor one giving ten percent of their insufficient income to charity is more generous than a rich one giving half of their wealth without impact to their own life.

*Generosity* is practiced by first practicing *altruism*, then considering one's own circumstances compared to others. It is nearly impossible not to find someone else as much or more in need than oneself. Continue in contentment, and express compassion for others in need, sharing with them in abundance, however limited that may be, without expectation for anything in return.

> ## Hospitality
>
> Hospitality is a special expression of generosity most often associated with sharing one's fundamental security—home, provisions, and personal attention. Hospitality captures additional behaviors like altruism, compassion, kindness, and gentleness, adding a personal flair which makes all those behaviors more meaningful to the recipient.

## Purpose – Flourish

Personal betterment and loving human relationships in truth are the end game for human flourishing, rolled up in the practices of *excellence* and *goodness*. These practices sum up and exemplify all the other Truth Practices and, being practically impossible to objectively achieve, provide a continuing challenge for betterment in truth. More importantly, practicing *excellence* and *goodness* in the other Truth Practices, and in all aspects of life, signifies that one is thriving in truth.

### *Practice – Excellence*

*Excellence* is a quality of superiority in something, whereas mediocrity is the norm. While natural individual talent can aid in developing excellence, talent is not equal to excellence because talent provides no benefit when left unexercised. Just as a fruit is excellent to eat when picked ripe, if left on the tree, it rots and benefits no one.

Excellence requires motivation, which comes from desire, discipline in gratitude, and wisdom to ensure sound purpose. Absent these, the excellent performance may be driven by foolish reasons or feelings of inadequacy. It may feel wonderful to excel at bending paper clips until they break or to please the domineering parent, but such excellence may be unwise, not providing value or happiness, and costing the opportunity to excel at something else that may be of more value.

Excellence serves both the excellent person and the people around them. Excellence motivates the desire for excellence in others, and as excellence becomes the norm (as past excellence becomes current mediocrity), greater excellence is achieved. This concept is perfectly clear in athletics and other activities in which records are kept. Records are regularly broken, which means that the objective standard of excellence is constantly being raised and the level of mediocrity along with it.

To practice *excellence*, practice all of the Truth Practices and resolve to improve in each one, each day—seeking excellence requires seeing every day as providing opportunity. Recover from failure of gratitude and courage, and continue in pursuit of personal betterment and human flourishing.

## *Practice – Goodness*

*Goodness* is the comprehensive quality of being and doing good—acting in truth for what is right, apart from foolishness, ignorance, and wickedness.

Most people believe they are good. Ask someone if they are good or not, and the likely response is, "I *consider myself* to be a good person." There is a reason why most do not say, "I *am* a good person." It is because, in the back of their mind, they are remembering all the times they were not a good person. Even if the initial response is, "I *am* a good person," many, if they take honest stock of their thoughts, actions, and beliefs, will find that they are not, on the whole, good.

Goodness is a peak of living to which to aspire. All humans are fallible. No one should expect to achieve perfection in life. No one is always good. Goodness is the overall state in which one seeks to do good and errs on the side of good, turning failures into learning and treating *goodness* as a practice of *excellence*. In that practice of excellence, gratitude drives one to seek to do good, having been the recipient of the goodness and blessing, and wisdom leads one to do good knowing that it is at the root of truth.

# Human Flourishing

The term *human flourishing* has been used throughout this book with little definition but always as a superlative, representing a superior state of things. And that is just what flourishing is—thriving, prospering, exceptional improvement.

*Flourishing* is often used as a description of plant growth in optimal conditions—fertile soil, the right amount of water, and proper sunlight to aid in sustained and exceptional growth and production, whether production be defined as beauty, seed, fruit, or raw material.

In human flourishing, Truth and its principles are the fertile soil, and society and civilization are the water and proper sunlight. It takes all beneficial conditions for flourishing. Survival is possible in less-than-optimal conditions, but when the necessary conditions are met—

establishing civilization based in Truth—humanity flourishes.

Society (including family) and civilization provide the total opportunity for application of Truth Principles in human relationships. In the natural order, culture and law drive society. In the spiritual order, gratitude and virtue lead society into civilization. Civilization leads to human flourishing. This reality becomes clearer when the potential states of society and civilization are charted based on the level of truth they support.

## Society

Liberty with duty—that is culture—are key indicators of the quality (or lack of quality) of a society. The Culture quadrant chart (page 111) demonstrates this relationship. When both liberty and duty are lacking in a culture (lower-left quadrant), that culture is subject to the most egregious breaches of humanity, which can be characterized as slavery, whether that slavery be of the body or of the mind.

Where liberty is limited but duty is required (lower-right quadrant), there is authoritarianism—control by authority without concern for the individual. Duty under authoritarianism takes many forms—from an indoctrinated, exaggerated, personal sense of duty (like "unquestioning fealty to the Fatherland") to "duty" imposed by force, which equates to slavery.

# Human Flourishing

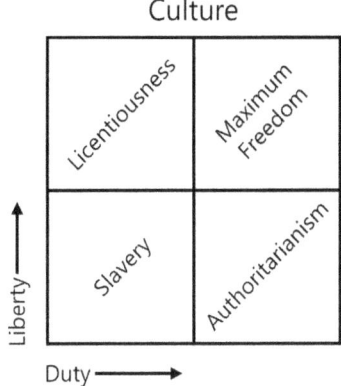

When duty is of little importance in a culture, and the sense of liberty is high (upper-left quadrant), licentiousness dominates. Such systemic licentiousness is more than simply "overdoing" liberty to a point where two liberties conflict but are readily mitigated thought negotiation or arbitration. A culture of licentiousness exhibits regular and wanton breach of duty and obligation to others. Such licentiousness may go so far as to become a threat to the property and lives of others. In this case, there is actually less freedom under licentiousness than under reasonable authority even though licentiousness represents itself as unlimited liberty. Only when both duty and liberty are strong in a culture (upper-right quadrant) does that culture achieve the maximum amount of freedom.

Similarly, administration of justice with mercy represents the rule of law in society as shown in the Law quadrant

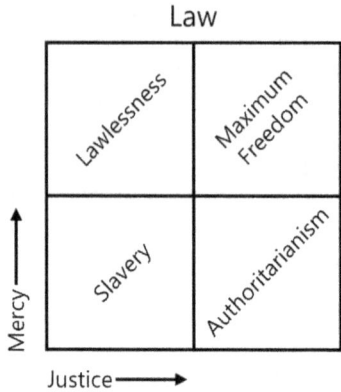

chart (page 112). Without justice and mercy, law devolves into slavery (lower-left quadrant), or into lawlessness (upper-left quadrant) if the administration of justice tolerates unlawful acts or misapplies justice or mercy.

With no mercy but much justice comes authoritarianism (lower-right quadrant). Justice, in this sense, is absolute in accord with the law (which may not be right law), and lack of mercy tends to increase the harshness of judgments over time, spiraling authoritarianism into totalitarianism—subjugation under absolute authority. Maximum freedom is only supported by maximum justice with appropriate mercy.

Combined, the Culture and Law quadrant charts represent the significant potential states of human society: Slavery, Licentiousness and Lawlessness—which is Anarchy, Authoritarianism, and Freedom. Slavery is an untenable state for any enlightened society. Eventually, the system will collapse in economic failure or rebellion. A licentious society is necessarily lawless, and where there is lawlessness, licentiousness will grow, resulting in anarchy. Anarchy presents a constant state of personal and societal danger and will quickly become authoritarian as the people seek security, and power consolidates under strong leaders, good or bad—historically bad (this is F.A. Hayek's "strong man" in *The Road to Serfdom* (24)). Mature authoritarianism—whether governed by fascism, socialism, or another form—may appear on the surface as a free society but is really just a shadow of free society because there is no individual liberty, only government-approved actions (and beliefs), and no natural duty, only government-prescribed actions. Maximum freedom—strong justice, mercy, liberty, and duty—is the optimum state for a thriving society as exemplified by modern representative republics (such as the United States of America) and free democracies.

The Society quadrant chart (page 114) highlights the precarious nature of society. With just one natural order principle (justice, mercy, liberty, duty) out of balance, society struggles to stay clear of authoritarianism, anarchy, and slavery.

The commonality of the influence of culture and law on the state of society means it is not practical to have good law with justice and mercy if the culture abandons duty or exercises licentiousness, and it is not tolerable to have bad law with righteous culture. In such cases, there will be a conflict between culture and law until one dominates and the loser is redefined to support the winner.

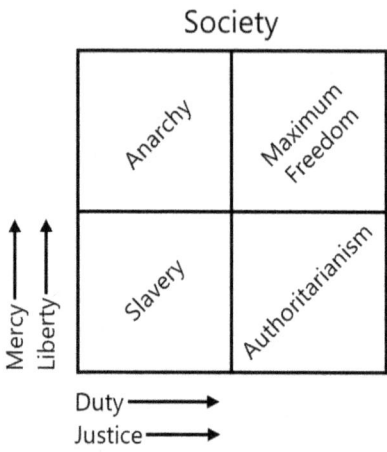

## Civilization

Civilization is the expansion of society to a superior level of organization and achievement—individually and collectively—driven by freedom in truth. C.S. Lewis implied the imperative for truth to uphold free society and civilization when he declared,

> A dogmatic belief in the objective value [truth] is necessary to the very idea of a rule [government] which is not tyranny or an obedience which is not slavery. (10 p. 73)

Slavery, authoritarianism, and anarchy are not civilization because slavery is the antithesis of civilization, authoritarianism merely pretends at being civilization by

*Human Flourishing* 115

creating its own "truth" rather than being built on Truth, and anarchy provides no formal society whatsoever until it falls into authoritarianism or slavery.

This understanding of civilization aligns with the state of maximum freedom in society, allowing the state of civilization to be overlayed on the Society quadrant chart—the upper-right quadrant of the Society chart overlapping with the lower-left quadrant of a Civilization chart—with the lower-left "worst case" of civilization being shared with the maximum freedom state of a society (page 116). Note that even in free society there may be a level of subsistence beneath the threshold required for civilization, so the lowest state of civilization is shifted above the minimum state of freedom in society. Put simply, a thriving free society is the minimum requirement for civilization.

The added axes of the Civilization quadrant chart are Virtue and Gratitude. Any degree of civilization supporting gratitude and virtue adds to human flourishing, so while there may be different expressions of civilization, there are no quadrant labels delineating types of civilization with more or less gratitude and virtue, and there is no such thing as too much gratitude or virtue in support of human flourishing. While the worst case of free society may leave some people in subsistence, in civilization, there are means and opportunity for more.

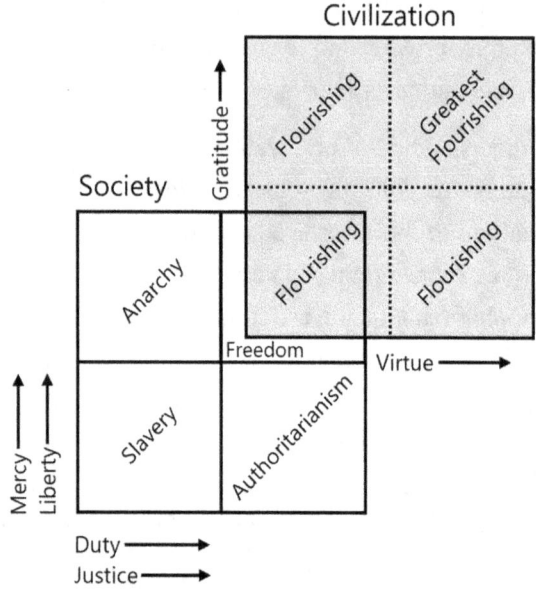

The benefit to civilization of more gratitude and more virtue is ever-expanding freedom and flourishing with less potential for a fall into anarchy or authoritarianism. As civilization increases, the practice of *gratitude* and *virtue* behaviors—*compassion, forgiveness, service, kindness, gentleness, goodness, generosity*, and more—extends flourishing to reach those who would be impoverished in simple society. In a grateful and virtuous civilization, those people who are in need receive provision and care rooted in the culture and find their own opportunity for individual betterment.

It should be a great encouragement to recognize that the same practices that make individuals better are also the practices that enhance society and enable civilization. It means that the more people who choose individual betterment, the more likely that others will prosper. This is the virtuous circle, and its natural process can be supercharged by those who know truth and who choose to learn and actively promote the practice of truth.

# The Source of Truth

Truth-Based Learning is structured so that elements of Truth may be practiced without fully understanding the source of Truth, but only when one seeks the source of Truth will the full impact of the principles and practices of Truth manifest in one's life and optimize human flourishing in society and civilization.

Truth must have a source. Yet, as Aristotle reasoned, "The principles of eternal things should be always most true (12)," meaning that truth is also eternal. So, eternal truth may only arise from an eternal source. Mankind is not eternal; therefore, Truth does not originate from mankind. The best that mankind can do is to seek truth and gather to it.

To begin the search for the source of Truth, examine the history of mankind. Long-term adherence to truth will positively correlate with the extent of civilization and human flourishing throughout time. The greatest extent of human flourishing—individually and collectively—the world has known came through Western Civilization, and the lasting source of Truth within Western Civilization is God—the God of the Bible; the God of Abraham, Isaac, and Jacob; God, the Father of Jesus Christ.

There is only one author of Truth, and that is God. God is Truth. Because God is Truth, there can be only one God, not many gods nor alternate gods because they could not all be "eternal things most true." The "Big Bang" did not create truth. God is the creator of all things, including Truth, including mankind.

Truth is an expression of the character of God. This is why the practices of Truth lead to good human character and why events in the lives of people, both natural and spiritual, expose elements of the whole Truth of God beyond that which can be reasoned or even imagined. However, the mere presence of spiritual practices in life does not mean that one may just choose their "preferred metaphysics" and call it truth from God. "My metaphysics," or "my spirituality," is no better than "my truth."

This is exemplified in a contemporary essay which defines God so as not, in the author's mind, to be controversial. The author calls God, "the Love and Intelligence that is the fabric of the universe and to which we are all connected (25)." While very poetical, and rightly ascribing love and intelligence to God, the uninspiring god imagined is just an experience to be had to bring people together—like having a picnic. Such limited definition and understanding of God stunts one's ability to understand truth. Assent to the need for a god is the beginning of understanding truth, but seeking truth eventually necessitates acceptance of God—agreement and alignment with the authority of God in all things, including truth.

Christianity is the imperfect human expression of the overarching spirituality (religion) of Western Civilization, which carries and sustains, in right discernment and application of the Bible, the perfect Truth of God. Mankind's religion has at times misinterpreted and corrupted spiritual truth in foolishness, ignorance, and wickedness. Yet, Truth remains. Christianity—turning from sin (sin is "missing the mark") and placing steadfast faith in Jesus Christ for forgiveness and reconciliation with God and the promise of resurrection after death to eternal life with God—is a practice of truth. And God, through Jesus Christ, is the author of Truth—Jesus said, "If you continue in My word, then you are truly My disciples; and you will know the truth, and the truth will set you free" (John 8:31-32).

# References

1. **Young, Toby.** A Classical Liberal Education. *The Telegraph.* [Online] Mar. 11, 2016. [Cited: Nov. 9, 2023.] Accessible on the Internet Archive Wayback Machine. https://web.archive.org/web/20160311201240/http://blogs.telegraph.co.uk/news/tobyyoung/100213007/a-classical-liberal-education/.

2. **Rush, Benjamin.** *Essays, Literary, Moral and Philosophical.* 2. Philadelphia : Thomas and William Bradford, 1806. p. 7. https://books.google.com/books?id=xtUKAAAAIAAJ&pg=PA7.

3. **Aurelius, Marcus.** *Meditations.* [trans.] Maxwell Staniforth. New York : Penguin Group, 2005. ISBN 978-0-14-303627-2.

4. **Burke, Edmund.** Several Scattered Hints Concerning Philosophy and Learning Collected Here from My Papers. *Econ Journal Watch.* [Online] Sep. 2022. [Cited: Nov. 9, 2023.] https://econjwatch.org/File+download/1234/BurkeSept2022.pdf?mimetype=pdf.

5. **Coolidge, Calvin.** American Education for America's Future. [ed.] A. E. Winship. *Journal of Education.* Aug. 25, 1921, Vol. 94, 6, pp. 143-146. https://books.google.com/books?id=K0E6AQAAMAAJ&pg=RA1-PA143.

6. **More, Thomas.** *Utopia.* [trans.] Dominic Baker-Smith. s.l. : Penguin Classics, 2020. ISBN 978-0-241-38268-4.

7. **Continental Congress of the United States of America.** Declaration of Independence. *Library of Congress.* [Online] Jul. 4, 1776. [Cited: Nov. 9, 2023.] https://www.loc.gov/resource/rbc0001.2004pe76546/.

8. **Alcoholics Anonymous.** The Twelve Steps. *Alcoholics Anonymous.* [Online] [Cited: Nov. 10, 2023.] https://www.aa.org/the-twelve-steps.

9. **McCosh, James.** *The Laws of Discursive Thought: Being a Text-book of Formal Logic.* New York : R. Carter & Brothers, 1873. p. 188. https://books.google.com/books?id=8uyVZzoW1FMC&pg=PA188.

10. **Lewis, C.S.** *The Abolition of Man.* New York : HarperCollins, 2001. Text (c) 1944. ISBN 978-0-06-065294-4.

11. **Kipling, Rudyard.** The Gods of the Copybook Headings. *The Kipling Society.* [Online] Oct. 26, 1919. [Cited: Nov. 9, 2023.] https://www.kiplingsociety.co.uk/poem/poems_copybook.htm.

12. **Aristotle.** *The Metaphysics of Aristotle: Translated from the Greek with Copious Notes in which the Pythagoric and Platonic Dogmas Respecting Numbers and Ideas are Unfolded from Ancient Sources...* London : Davis, Wilks, and Taylor, 1801. p. 36. Bekker Number: Metaphysics 2.993b30-31, https://books.google.com/books?id=oCBdAAAAMAAJ&pg=PA36.

13. —. *The Metaphysics of Aristotle: Translated from the Greek with Copious Notes in which the Pythagoric and Platonic Dogmas Respecting Numbers and Ideas are Unfolded from Ancient Sources...* [trans.] Thomas Taylor. London : Davis, Wilks, and Taylor, 1801. p. 105. Bekker Number: Metaphysics 4.1011b25, https://books.google.com/books?id=oCBdAAAAMAAJ&pg=PA105.

14. **Gregory, James Monroe.** *Frederick Douglass the Orator: Containing an Account of His Life; His Eminent Public Services; His Brilliant Career as Orator;*

*Selections from His Speeches and Writings.* s.l. : Willey & Company, 1893. p. 36.
https://books.google.com/books?id=QmUNDiaCV68C&pg=PA101.

15. **Aristotle.** *The Nicomachean Ethics of Aristotle.* [ed.] Robert William Browne. [trans.] Robert William Browne. London : Henry G. Bohn, 1853. pp. 240-241. https://books.google.com/books?id=9vjZkQXrOcoC&pg=PA240, Bekker Number Nic. Eth. 9.4.

16. **Locke, John.** *Two Treatises of government.* London : Awnsham and John Churchill at the Black Swan, 1698. p. 301.
https://books.google.com/books?id=7kwUAAAAQAAJ&pg=PA301.

17. **Stanford University.** Critical Thinking. *Stanford Encyclopedia of Philosophy.* [Online] Oct. 12, 2022. [Cited: Nov. 9, 2023.]
https://plato.stanford.edu/entries/critical-thinking/#DefiCritThin.

18. **Blackstone, William.** *An Analysis of the Laws of England.* 6. Oxford : Clarendon Press, 1771. pp. 2-4. https://books.google.com/books?id=Q8sDAAAAQAAJ&pg=PA2.

19. **Elliot, Elisabeth.** *Through Gates of Splendor.* New York : Harper & Brothers, 1957. Library of Congress number 57-7341.

20. **Jerumbo, Autumn.** How to Be a Good AA Sponsor. *Alcoholics Anonymous.* [Online] [Cited: Nov. 9, 2023.] https://alcoholicsanonymous.com/what-makes-a-good-aa-sponsor/.

21. **Covey, Stephen R.** *The 7 Habits of Highly Successful People.* New York : s.n., 1989. ISBN 0-671-70863-5.

22. **Solzhenitsyn, Aleksandr.** Live Not By Lies. *The Aleksandr Solzhenitsyn Center.* [Online] Feb. 12, 1974. [Cited: Nov. 9, 2023.] https://www.solzhenitsyncenter.org/live-not-by-lies.

23. **Strong, James.** *The Exhaustive Concordance of the Bible: Showing Every Word of the Text of the Common English Version of the Canonical Books, and Every Occurrence of Each Word in Regular Order; Together with A Comparative Concordance of the Authorized and Revised Version.* New York : Hunt & Eaton, 1894. p. 65. https://books.google.com/books?id=3TBGAQAAMAAJ&pg=RA3-PA65.

24. **Hayek, F. A.** The Road to Serfdom in Cartoons. *Mises Institute.* [Online] 1945. [Cited: Nov. 9, 2023.] https://cdn.mises.org/Road%20to%20Serfdom%20in%20Cartoons.pdf.

25. **Brownstein, Barry.** RFK Jr. vs. The Man of System, Part 2. *Mindset Shifts—Essays by Barry Brownstein.* [Online] Substack, Oct. 13, 2023. [Cited:

Nov. 9, 2023.] https://mindsetshifts.substack.com/p/rfk-jr-vs-the-man-of-system-part-47f.

# Biblical References

Christianity is the expression of the overarching spirituality of Western Civilization. In that light, much of the discussion in this book relates to Judeo-Christian concepts and principles from the Bible. Some of those relationships have already been referenced, but many are implicit in the discussion and are listed here for those interested in reviewing the biblical connections. This list is not exhaustive; more references are possible as a quick review of the book of Proverbs would attest.

| Page | Biblical Reference |
| --- | --- |
| 5 | Mark 6:3, |
| | Matthew 7:28-29, |
| | Matthew 21, |
| | Romans 8:34 |
| 9 | Proverbs 14:12 |
| 16 | Genesis 4:8-14 |

| Page | Biblical Reference |
|---|---|
| 17 | Exodus 20:3-717, Romans 2:14-15 |
| 19 | John 18:38 |
| 22 | 1 John 2:21, Matthew 12:25, Matthew 12:30, Matthew 12:33 |
| 27 | Isaiah 5:20 |
| 28 | 2 Thessalonians 2:10 |
| 29 | Proverbs 3:35, Proverbs 18:2, Proverbs 28:26 |
| 35 | Mark 12:31 |
| 36 | Ephesians 5:28 |
| 37 | 1 Corinthians 13:4-7, 1 John 4:19, Galatians 5:22, John 15:13, Philippians 2:3 |
| 38 | John 11:36, Luke 10:30-37, Romans 12:10 |
| 40 | 2 Timothy 3:2, Colossians 3:14, Ephesians 5:29, Leviticus 19:18, Matthew 22:39 |

## Biblical References

| Page | Biblical Reference |
|---|---|
| 41 | Exodus 20:12, Genesis 2:23-24 |
| 43 | James 3:1 |
| 49 | Galatians 5:13 |
| 52 | Matthew 7:12 |
| 54 | Colossians 4:6, Mark 9:50 |
| 55 | 1 Peter 1:17, James 2:9, Leviticus 19:15, Proverbs 24:23 |
| 56 | 2 Corinthians 5:17 |
| 58 | Matthew 27:16-26 |
| 59 | John 1:17 |
| 63 | Proverbs 6:6-8 |
| 65 | Acts 17:23 |
| 66 | 1 Corinthians 15:33 |
| 77 | James 1:22 |
| 79 | Romans 2:11 |
| 81 | Luke 10:27-37 |
| 87 | Romans 15:13 |
| 88 | Proverbs 19:24 |
| 93 | Proverbs 16:18 |
| 97 | Proverbs 19:11 |
| 101 | Philippians 4:5 |
| 103 | Philippians 2:4 |

| Page | Biblical Reference |
|---|---|
| 105 | Hebrews 13:2, Leviticus 19:33-34, Philippians 4:8 |
| 107 | Ephesians 2:10, Galatians 6:9, Galatians 6:10, Romans 12:9 |
| 119 | Genesis 3:19 |
| 120 | 1 Timothy 2:3-4, Exodus 3:6, John 14:6, John 14:9, Numbers 23:19, Proverbs 30:5 |
| 121 | John 1:3, John 8:31-32 |

# Index

*agape*, 36
Alcoholics Anonymous, 16, 85
anarchy, 112
*argumentum ad populum*, 18
Aristotle, 21, 39, 119
Aurelius, Marcus, 8, 14, 38
authoritarianism, 79, 112
Blackstone, William, 59
body of knowledge, 17
body of wisdom, 19
Burke, Edmund, 8
character, 77
Christianity, 121
civilization, 11, 114
classical liberal education, 4
clemency, 58
common sense, 20
complacency, 88
Coolidge, Calvin, 10
*corpus sapiens*, 19
*corpus scientiae*, 17
creativity, 54
critical thinking, 47
culture, 52
Declaration of Independence, 14, 24, 96
discernment, 43
disinformation, 30
diversity, 80
Douglass, Frederick, 22
Dunning-Kruger effect, 18
education, 1
*eros*, 36
facts, 30
fairness, 57
Golden Rule, 52, 66
grace, 104

habit, 85, 86
Hayek, F.A., 113
honor, 68
hope, 87
hospitality, 105
human flourishing, 109
influencer, 42
integrity, 78
Jesus Christ, 37, 120, 121
journalism, 46
joy, 87
law, 59
Laws of Nature, 14, 45
Laws of Nature's God, 14, 16, 45
Lewis, C.S., 19, 20, 25, 114
licentiousness, 49, 111, 112
Locke, John, 14, 45
Media, 42, 46
mediocrity, 105
meekness, 101
narrative, 42, 46
Natural Law, 14, 60
natural order, 14
offense, 93
patience, 95, 97
peace, 87
persistence, 64, 85
personality, 54
*philautia*, 36
*philia*, 36
Pollyannaism, 65, 66
popular culture, 20, 53

Practice
  Altruism, 103
  Compassion, 100
  Contentment, 87
  Courage, 94
  Discipline, 84
  Dutifulness, 81
  Excellence, 105
  Forbearance, 97
  Forgiveness, 88
  Generosity, 104
  Gentleness, 100
  Goodness, 107
  Honesty, 94
  Humility, 90
  Justness, 82
  Kindness, 102
  Long-suffering, 95
  Respect for Life, 78
  Self-Control, 83
  Steadfastness, 97
pride, 90, 93
priming, 46
Principle
  Duty, 49
  Equality, 61
  Gratitude, 63
  Justice, 54
  Liberty, 49
  Love, 35
  Mercy, 54
  Virtue, 66
  Wisdom, 42
propaganda, 46
Purpose
  Appreciate Others, 74

Choose Betterment, 83
Examine Self, 74
Find Right Sense of Self, 87
Flourish, 105
Hone Relationships, 95
Live as a Citizen, 78
Resolve to Defend Truth, 91
Sacrifice for Others, 102
Value Others, 99
reason, 45
scientific method, 26, 30
slavery, 110
society, 110
Solzhenitsyn, Aleksandr, 91
spiritual order, 14
*storge*, 36
thankfulness, 64
tolerance, 99
Utopia, 13
vicious cycle, 41
virtuous circle, 6, 9, 41, 117
Western Civilization, 12, 31, 120, 121
wisdom of crowds, 17
*zeitgeist*, 53

www.ingramcontent.com/pod-product-compliance
Lightning Source LLC
Chambersburg PA
CBHW050224100526
44585CB00017BA/1977